Jesus the Healer

Jesus the Healer

Darrell W. Johnson

Regent College Publishing
www.regentpublishing.com

Jesus the Healer
Copyright © 2017 Darrell W. Johnson

Published 2017 by Regent College Publishing

Regent College Publishing
5800 University Boulevard, Vancouver, BC V6T 2E4 Canada
Web: www.regentpublishing.com
E-mail: info@regentpublishing.com

Regent College Publishing is an imprint of the Regent Book-
store <www.regentbookstore.com>. Views expressed in works
published by Regent College Publishing are those of the author
and do not necessarily represent the official position of Regent
College <www.regent-college.edu>.

ISBN 978-1-57383-539-8

Cataloguing in Publication information is on file at Library and
Archives Canada.

To three (among so many!) of His disciples
Jesus used to bring me His healing:

Presbyterian pastor Robert Whittaker,
who prayed for healing of fear;

Clinical psychologist Archibald Hart,
who taught me the mind-body nexus
and its implications for depression and stress;

Medical doctor Joy Liao,
who embodies Jesus's wholistic healing ministry,
helping me recover from a heart-attack.

Thank you!

CONTENTS

Acknowledgments   ix

Introduction   xi

1. Preaching, Teaching, Healing   1

2. If You Are Willing   23

3. Just Say the Word   41

4. He Takes and Carries   52

5. Even the Wind and the Waves   69

6. One Little Word Shall Fell Him   82

7. Authority to Forgive   102

8. Faith in the Valley of the Shadow of Death   115

9. Just Keep Following Him Home   132

10. Joining Jesus the Healer   145

   Afterword   159

   He Gives Us a New Past!   161

   Questions for Small Group Studies   179

   For Further Reading   187

Acknowledgments

There are a number of people I would like to acknowledge who helped get this material into book form. In addition to the Biblical scholars and theologians I quote throughout, I want to thank those who turned my increasingly difficult to read hand written manuscripts into legible pages: Sofie Asa, who served me as secretary at Union Church of Manila; Lou Foley, who served me in the similar capacity at Fremont Presbyterian Church in Sacramento; Beth Malena, who collated my teaching notes at Regent College; and Doug Liao (nee Hills) who pulled all the various forms of the teaching together while serving me at First Baptist in Vancouver. And I want to thank the team at Regent Publishing for their expert editing and Oliver Hung, my present assistant for then helping me complete the final version. Any remaining mistakes are, of course, mine. I am blessed to have been so graciously served!

Introduction

Many of us who were raised in North America grew up hearing and reciting nursery rhymes. I would guess that those of you who were raised in other parts of the world grew up with similar poems or songs.

One of my favorites was "Humpty-Dumpty." It is about an egg-shaped fellow who has a nasty, catastrophic fall.

> Humpty Dumpty sat on a wall.
> Humpty Dumpty had a great fall.
> All the king's horses and all the king's men,
> Couldn't put Humpty together again.

Every time I heard the rhyme I felt sad, for it seemed to me that Humpty's experience was the experience of the whole human race. We have had a great fall, and none of us has been able to put us together again.

Well, I have good news for Humpty Dumpty—and for every human being who knows the pain of brokenness and who longs to be made whole. Actually, the Bible has good news for Humpty and all of us who feel what he feels. There is a King who can put us together again. Indeed, a King who can put the whole created order together again!

We read about Him and His work all over the pages of the four Gospels in the New Testament. But we especially read about Him putting things together again in the Gospel according to Matthew. In chapters eight and nine, Matthew, the tax-collector turned evangelist, records ten examples of King Jesus entering into our brokenness and bringing about substantive levels of healing. And people are amazed and begin to bring to Jesus friends and neighbors in all kinds of need. And He heals them!

In this book are sermons I have preached, in a number of contexts around the world, on Jesus' deeds in Matthew 8-9. In each sermon I seek to understand what Matthew claims Jesus did. I then grapple with what it means for us 2,000 years later.

But before moving into the deeds themselves, let us consider two texts which "bracket" the deeds. Let us work through the way Matthew sets up and wraps up the King's healing work.

JESUS
the Healer

1

Preaching, Teaching, Healing

Matthew 4:12-17, 23-25; 9:35-10:1

4:12Now when Jesus heard that John had been taken into custody, He withdrew into Galilee; 13and leaving Nazareth, He came and settled in Capernaum, which is by the sea, in the region of Zebulun and Naphtali. 14This was to fulfill what was spoken through Isaiah the prophet:

> *15"The land of Zebulun and the land of Naphtali,*
> *By the way of the sea, beyond the Jordan,*
> *   Galilee of the Gentiles—*
> *16"The people who were sitting in darkness*
> *   saw a great Light,*
> *And those who were sitting in the land*
> *   and shadow of death,*
> *Upon them a Light dawned."*

17From that time Jesus began to preach and say, "Repent, for the kingdom of heaven is at hand." . . .

23 Jesus was going throughout all Galilee, teaching in their synagogues and proclaiming the gospel of the kingdom, and healing every kind of disease and every kind of sickness among the people.

24 The news about Him spread throughout all Syria; and they brought to Him all who were ill, those suffering with various diseases and pains, demoniacs, epileptics, paralytics; and He healed them. 25 Large crowds followed Him from Galilee and the Decapolis and Jerusalem and Judea and from beyond the Jordan. . . .

9:35 Jesus was going through all the cities and villages, teaching in their synagogues and proclaiming the gospel of the kingdom, and healing every kind of disease and every kind of sickness.

36 Seeing the people, He felt compassion for them, because they were distressed and dispirited like sheep without a shepherd. 37 Then He said to His disciples, "The harvest is plentiful, but the workers are few. 38 Therefore beseech the Lord of the harvest to send out workers into His harvest."

10:1 Jesus summoned His twelve disciples and gave them authority over unclean spirits, to cast them out, and to heal every kind of disease and every kind of sickness.

PREACHING, TEACHING . . .

According to Matthew the tax-collector-turned-Gospel-writer, the earthly ministry of Jesus of Nazareth is one of preaching, teaching, and healing. According to Matthew, the Risen Jesus has entrusted the same three-fold ministry to His disciples. As you can hear and see in these texts, Matthew is careful to keep the three verbs together. He keeps them together because Jesus's teaching, preaching and healing involve the same reality.

Jesus came preaching what? What was His basic message, His gospel? "Repent [turn around], for the kingdom of heaven is at hand" (Matt. 4:17).

"The time is fulfilled" (Mark 1:15). The word translated "time" is the Greek word *kairos*. The more usual Greek word for "time" is the word *kronos*, which comes into the English language in words like "chronology" and "chronological." "*Kronos*-time" is, as my uncle Emmett used to put it, "tick-tock" time that can be measured by clocks and calendars. "*Kairos*-time," however, cannot be measured by clocks and calendars. It involves unique moments in "*kronos*-time" when the Living God decides to act in fulfillment of promise.

Jesus came preaching, "The *kairos* is fulfilled"! Jesus came announcing that it was time for God to move in a new and unprecedented way. History had reached a crisis point. In Jesus, that unique, decisive moment for the fulfillment of God's great promises has begun. Dutch scholar Herman Ridderbos said it so well: Jesus came announcing that "the threshold of the great future has been reached . . . the concluding drama can start."[1]

And what is the concluding drama? Jesus came preaching that the *kairos* is fulfilled; the kingdom of heaven is at hand; the kingdom of God has come near. It is time for heaven to invade the earth! It is time for the future, God's great future, to spill into the present.[2]

In and because of Jesus, the glorious rule of God, which was thought to come only at the end of history, is breaking into the middle of history. It is *kairos* time. This is why we hear Jesus use the word "today" so much:

> In His synagogue sermon in Nazareth:
> "Today this Scripture has been fulfilled in your hearing" (Luke 4:21).

> At a dinner party with Zaccheus the tax collector:
> "Today salvation has come to this house" (Luke 19:9).

> On the cross to the dying thief:
> "Today you shall be with Me in Paradise" (Luke 23:43).

Today, in Me . . . the kingdom has come near.

This is the message Jesus preached throughout the cities and villages of Galilee and Judea. This is the

---

[1] Herman Ridderbos, *The Coming of the Kingdom* (Philadelphia: Presbyterian and Reformed, 1962), 48.

[2] For more information, see George E. Ladd, *The Presence of the Future: The Eschatology of Biblical Realism* (Grand Rapids: Eerdmans, 1974).

good news Jesus announced to people whom Matthew, quoting the prophet Isaiah, characterizes as "sitting in the land and shadow of death" (4:16). Jesus came preaching that in Him Light has dawned! It is time for God's rule of Light and Life to invade the rule of darkness and death! And what happened on Easter morning validated Jesus's gospel. Jesus, alive after being crucified, says that He was right—the kingdom of God has indeed come near!

So Jesus came preaching, but also teaching. Jesus came teaching the nature of the kingdom breaking into the world. Many of Jesus's parables begin, "The kingdom is like . . . " To be in the kingdom of God is to share in the life of God, to be drawn into the inner life of God. In His famous Sermon on the Mount, Jesus unfolds the relational and ethical nature of the kingdom, describing the new character traits and new life styles of those upon whom the Light has dawned, in whom the life of God is being lived.

. . . AND HEALING

Jesus came preaching and teaching . . . and healing. Why? Why did He come healing? The answer is crucial to grasp. Jesus came healing because the kingdom whose nearness He declares and whose nature He explains is all about the restoration of human life—and the restoration of the universe!

This is what gave great hope and joy to the prophets of old, especially to Isaiah. Listen to his vision of the future:

Say to those with anxious heart,
 "Take courage, fear not.
 Behold, your God will come. . . ."
Then the eyes of the blind will be opened
 And the ears of the deaf will be unstopped.
Then the lame will leap like a dear,
And the tongue of the mute will shout for joy.
For waters will break forth in the wilderness
And streams in the Arabah. (Isa. 35:4-6)

In His acts of healing, Jesus is manifesting the very reality He is preaching and teaching. Jesus of Nazareth is the bringer of the kingdom. He restores human lives *not* to prove that fact, but because the kingdom He bears is the kingdom of wholeness. The reign of God is all about putting people together again. This is why Hans Küng says, "God's kingdom is creation healed."[3]

The need for Jesus's gospel is clear enough, is it not? The wreckage is all around us. In the words of Eugene Peterson: "wrecked bodies, wrecked marriages, wrecked careers, wrecked plans, wrecked families, wrecked alliances, wrecked friendships, wrecked prosperity."[4] Are there not times when you, like me, feel overwhelmed by the sheer magnitude of the need?

This is the gospel according to Jesus: in Him the

[3] Hans Küng, *On Being a Christian*, trans. Edward Quinn (Garden City, NY: Doubleday, 1976), 231.
[4] Eugene H. Peterson, *Working the Angles: The Shape of Pastoral Integrity* (Grand Rapids: Eerdmans, 1987), 15.

Living God comes into the midst of the mess to repair, restore, and recreate every dimension of human existence. This is what salvation is all about; this is what we are affirming when we call Jesus "Saviour." The words "salvation" and "Saviour" are related to the Hebrew word *shalom*. And *shalom* means soundness, wholenesss, well-being.

Yes, to be saved means to be rescued from the consequences of sin, to be rescued from condemnation and death. But to be saved means also, and primarily, to be made whole again, to be restored to relationship with God, to relationship with others, to relationship with self, and to relationship with creation. To be saved is to experience "well-being" in all the dimensions of life.

For too long now the church, especially the church under the influence of Western Christianity, has missed this holistic nature of salvation because we have implicitly adopted a Greek view of what it means to be a human being. For the Greeks, a human being is a collection of separate parts: a collection of mind, body, soul, and spirit. In the Greek view of things, these parts can be isolated and can function apart from each other. Thus, for most of the ancient Greek thinkers, the body was basically unrelated to the mind and spirit. It was at best a nuisance, at worst a prison. The soul was all that mattered.

When Western Christianity preached the gospel, it did so out of a Greek view of humanity, and therefore preached less than the good news of Jesus Christ. "Jesus saves" came to mean "Jesus saves souls." Now that is true! But it is not the whole truth. The truth is "Jesus saves human beings," and human beings are more than souls.

In the Hebrew view of things a human being is a unitary reality. That is, body, soul, mind, and spirit are but different ways of speaking about the one same reality. For purposes of diagnosis they can be separated, but they can never be separated in practice—as doctors keep telling us! In the Hebrew view of things

> I do not have a body—I am a body.
> I do not have a soul—I am a soul.
> I do not have a mind—I am a mind.
> I do not have a spirit—I am a spirit.

I was created to be a physical-psychological-mental-spiritual whole.

The gospel is that Jesus Christ saves the whole of me: soul, mind, spirit, and body. I love the blessing the apostle Paul speaks over the people of Thessalonica: "Now may the God of peace [*shalom*] Himself sanctify you entirely; and may your spirit and soul and body be preserved complete, without blame at the coming of our Lord Jesus Christ" (1 Thess. 5:23).

> Jesus came preaching: "The kingdom of God has come near."
> Jesus came teaching: "The kingdom of God is like . . ."

Jesus came healing: manifesting the kingdom
in the midst of all the mess.

TEN DEEDS

Thus, between these two texts giving summaries of Jesus's ministry (Matt. 4 and Matt. 9), Matthew records the Sermon on the Mount and ten deeds of Jesus. In Matthew 5-7, Jesus speaks of loving our enemies, of blessing those who curse us, and of living free from anxiety: that is the kingdom of God come near. In Matthew 8-9, we find Jesus entering ten different expressions of human brokenness and putting things together again.

The ten deeds are concrete illustrations and expressions of Jesus's gospel. The ten deeds declare that God's new order is breaking into this world, and they anticipate what it will be like when the light finally drives the darkness away.

These ten mighty deeds of Jesus are the following:

Jesus touches a man with leprosy, and the man is cleansed of his disorder. That is the kingdom of God come near (8:1-4).

Jesus speaks healing to a Roman centurion's servant, "sight unseen." That, especially the fact that Jesus the Jew bothers with a Roman, is the kingdom of God come near (8:5-13).

Jesus touches the head of Peter's mother-in-law who has a severe fever and she is restored and begins to serve Jesus. That is the kingdom of God come near (8:14-17).

Jesus rebukes the winds and waves of a storm, and the sea becomes perfectly calm. That is the kingdom of God come near (8:23-27).

Jesus, simply by a word, releases two men from the grip of the demonic. That is the kingdom of God come near (8:28-34).

Four men break a hole in their neighbor's roof in order to lower their paralyzed friend to the feet of Jesus (cf. Luke 5:19). Jesus surprises them, saying "Take courage, son; your sins are forgiven," and then later, "Get up, pick up your bed and go home." That is the kingdom of God come near (9:1-8).

A synagogue official pleads with Jesus to come and lay His hands on his daughter who has just died. Jesus goes to the man's house, takes the girl by the hand and she comes to life! That is the kingdom of God come near (9:18-26).

A woman who has been hemorrhaging for twelve years sneaks up behind Jesus and touches the fringe of His robe. Jesus turns around and says to her, "Daughter, take courage; your faith has made you well." That is the kingdom of God come near (9:19-22).

Two men who are blind follow after Jesus crying out, "Have mercy on us, Son of David." Jesus touches their eyes saying, "It shall be done to you according to your faith." And they see! That is the kingdom of God come near (9:27-31).

A man who could not speak and who was demon-possessed was brought to Jesus. Jesus drives out the demonic power and the man speaks! That is the kingdom of God come near (9:32-34).

The entire career of Jesus of Nazareth is to be viewed through His announcement that "the *kairos* is fulfilled." Everything He does is a manifestation of the in-breaking of God's new world order.

And it is for this new order of wholeness that we are praying every time we say, "Our Father, who is in heaven . . . Your kingdom come . . . on earth as it is in heaven" (Matt. 6:9-10).

Now, all of this raises a host of questions, such as:

If Jesus's good news is true news, why do we not see it more?

If Jesus came to restore, why is there still so much brokenness?

We prayed our hearts out, yet nothing seemed to change; why did we not seem to get an answer?

I know we are all going to die one day; how
much kingdom wholeness can we realistically
expect this side of passing into the next life?

And most importantly for us as we seek to love
our city: what can we promise people who
come to Jesus with their brokenness?

In the coming chapters we will grapple with such
questions as we make our way through Matthew 8-9.
In this introductory chapter, let me briefly develop four
observations that can keep us on track, pointers that
keep us faithful to Jesus and His good news.

THE MYSTERY OF RESISTANCE

Pointer number one I will call "the mystery of resistance." I call it a "mystery" because in the final analysis I do
not understand why anyone would resist the in-breaking
of the kingdom. But we do. Not everyone wants Jesus to
bring in the rule of God. Indeed, most humans resist it.

We like the idea of creation being healed, but we resist
the fact that in order for that to happen we have to turn
around. "Repent" is the word Jesus uses. I have to turn
around, at a deep, deep level. I have to die to my desire
to rule my life. You see, the kingdom happens wherever
Jesus is allowed to be King. And in order for Him to be
King, I have to die to my own self-lordship. I have to stop,
make a U-turn of radical proportions, and surrender to
His claim upon my life. The mystery of resistance: deep
down we resist the very thing that sets us free.

Even when we do want the kingdom to come, we resist. To be healed means our lives will end up changing, and we resist change. If we are healed we may have to exercise new levels of responsibility. Is that not why Jesus asked the man who was lame for thirty-eight years, "Do you wish to get well?" (John 5:6) Of course he does! Or does he? There are certain benefits to remaining broken. People bring you meals, you don't have to go to work, you don't have to care about what is going on in the community, you don't have to try to be a nice person. "Do you want to get well?" Yes . . . and yet . . . we resist.

THE COMPLEXITY OF OUR HUMANITY

But what of those who really do want to get well, who accept all the consequent changes, yet still struggle? I call pointer number two "the complexity of our humanity." There are many dimensions to human brokenness. Often brokenness in one dimension is due to brokenness in another.

There is, of course, the physical dimension. But there is also the emotional and the relational and the spiritual. One's particular form of brokenness may be experienced in one dimension but be rooted in another. Doctors tell us that much of our physical illness is the symptom of emotional or relational or spiritual illness. How many times have we heard, "There is nothing structurally wrong with you"?

Jesus, the "Great Physician," can discern the root cause

of our specific forms of brokenness. And often, when it seems that no repair work is going on, He is working at another level. I am sure that the four men who brought their paralyzed friend to Jesus were at first disappointed when, instead of saying, "Your legs are healed," Jesus said, "Your sins are forgiven." What does that have to do with paralysis? Jesus discerned that although there may have been organic reasons for the illness, the root cause was spiritual. Jesus saw through to the deeper need and brought healing at that level first.

The King is working in each of us who has welcomed Him. He may not be working in the way we want Him to, but He *is* working. And what is true of us as individuals is true of us as families, churches, cities, and nations. He is at work, going after the deepest expressions of our brokenness.

THE TENSION IN JESUS'S GOSPEL

A third observation is the great tension inherent in Jesus's gospel. In His preaching Jesus uses the term "at hand" or "come near." "The kingdom of heaven is at hand." "The kingdom of God has come near."

Does Jesus mean it is just about to arrive, so get ready? Or does He mean it is right here, so grab hold of it? Yes—to both! In using the terms "at hand" and "come near," Jesus is pointing to a tension in His gospel, a tension which theologians call the "already, not-yet." I have spoken of this many times, and will continue to do so until the "not yet" is "already"!

In Jesus, God's kingdom of wholeness is already present in some form, but not yet present in the form it will be at the culmination of history. The fact that Jesus has already come and is with us says that something of God's kingdom has "already" come and is here. But the fact that Jesus teaches us to pray for the kingdom says there is something "not yet" still to come.

When we see or hear or say the phrase "Jesus heals" or "Jesus Christ repairs the wreckage," we need to remember that this Jesus is:

the Jesus of Christmas Eve,
the Jesus of Good Friday,
the Jesus of Easter,
the Jesus of Pentecost, and
the Jesus of the Apocalypse, of
the Second Coming.

That is:

the purpose of Jesus's birth is incomplete without
His life;
the purpose of Jesus's life is incomplete without
His death;
the purpose of Jesus's death is incomplete without
His resurrection;
the purpose of Jesus's resurrection is incomplete
without his ascension to the throne of God;
the purpose of Jesus's ascension is incomplete
without His pouring out of the Holy Spirit

upon the church; and
the purpose of Jesus's pouring out of the Spirit is
incomplete without His coming again in glory.

Because He has already come, the kingdom of wholeness has already come. But because He has not yet come, the kingdom of wholeness has not yet come. Faith is all about living in that tension.

The church has throughout the centuries tended to swing back and forth between two extremes. Either Christians have emphasized the "not-yet" to the exclusion of the "already," or Christians have emphasized the "already" to the exclusion of the "not-yet."

On the one hand, we are told that this is a broken world and that it will be that way until Jesus Christ comes again. In the meantime, we are to accept the brokenness and let God help us endure it with grace. On the other hand, we are told that total healing is now: "Just name it, and claim it."

We must resist both extremes, for the kingdom of wholeness is both already and not-yet. None of us will be completely whole until that day when "what is mortal will be swallowed up by life" (2 Cor. 5:4). Yet because "the *kairos* is fulfilled" something has happened, can happen, and is happening. The King is working to restore even now.

KEEP THE ISSUE CLEAR

This brings me to the fourth pointer, the most

important factor as we grapple with all the questions: Jesus. Keep your eyes on Jesus, who stands in the midst of the wreckage.

In Matthew 8 and 9, in the ten deeds, two things stand out about Jesus, and it is to these two things that Matthew consistently draws us. They are Jesus's authority and Jesus's compassion. Jesus has the authority of a King and the compassion of a Shepherd. Matthew keeps them together, and so must we. So, throw yourself on the authority and compassion of Jesus.

Jesus's Authority

In the ten deeds in Matthew 8 and 9 we see Jesus exercising authority over all the forces that threaten to undo us.

We see His authority over sin:
"Take courage, son; your sins are forgiven" (9:2).
We see His authority over disease:
"And immediately his leprosy was cleansed" (8:3).
We see His authority over the demonic:
"They came out" (8:32).
We see His authority over the chaotic forces of nature:
He "rebuked the winds and the sea" (8:26).
And we see His authority over death:
He "took her by the hand, and the girl got up" (9:25).

And Matthew emphasizes the fact that Jesus exercises his authority by His word. Jesus simply speaks and something happens!

To the man with leprosy:
> "I am willing; be cleansed" (8:3).
> And he was.

To the centurion:
> "Go; it shall be done for you as you have believed"
> "And the servant was healed that very moment"
> (8:13).

To the demons:
> "Go!" (8:32).
> And they ran.

To the paralytic:
> "Your sins are forgiven" (9:2).
> And he was.

Matthew intends for us to hear in Jesus's word the echo of the original creative word. We are to hear in Jesus's voice that voice which first spoke the world into being. The One who has entered our brokenness is the One who in the beginning said, "Let there be light" and there was! Jesus Christ need only speak, and something happens.

Am I overstating the case? Not at all. For what does Jesus say after His resurrection? "All authority has been given to Me in heaven and on earth" (Matt. 28:18). Jesus, the Word made flesh, had the first word, and He has the last word over everything. He need only say "Now!" and a new heaven and a new earth descends . . . and the glory of God fills the universe.

Jesus's Compassion

Throw yourself on Jesus's authority—and on His

18

compassion. One of the most powerful lines in Scripture is Matthew 9:36: "Seeing the people, He felt compassion for them, because they were distressed and dispirited like sheep without a shepherd."

The word Matthew uses is a deeply visceral word, which is too weakly translated as "felt compassion." It is the word splanchna, and refers to the inner parts of our bodies, to the seat of our most intense and tender emotions. It is translated in other places in the Bible as "bowels" or "guts." The splanchna are where we experience those emotions that clutch at us, that wrench and tear us apart. Matthew is saying, "Jesus saw the crowds and His guts were ripped up."

The bringer and bearer of the kingdom of wholeness is the Shepherd who feels the pain of the sheep. We can endure the "already, not-yet," and we can wait for His word of authority, when we know that the King feels the brokenness. He bleeds with us in our woundedness.

Jesus went to Bethany after Lazarus died, and when Jesus saw the tomb of His friend, He wept (John 11:35). Jesus knew what He was going to do; He was going to speak Lazarus out of the tomb back into life. But before He speaks, He weeps. The word John uses is another deeply visceral word, meaning to "snort in spirit." It is used to describe a horse rearing up on its hind legs, pawing at the air and snorting. Jesus saw the grave, and experienced gut-wrenching pain. It is one of the most mysterious moments in history: the incarnate God in pain.

So Henri Nouwen can say:

When Jesus was moved to compassion, the source of all life trembled, the ground of all love burst open, and the abyss of God's immense, inexhaustible, and unfathomable tenderness revealed itself.[5]

No one I know grasps this dimension of the gospel better than the Japanese theologian Kazoh Kitamori. His book, *Theology of the Pain of God,* was written in 1965 when Japanese Christians were finally emotionally able to wrestle with the dropping of the bombs on Hiroshima and Nagaski. In it, Kitamori wrote:

God in pain is the God who resolves our human pain by his own. Jesus Christ is the Lord who heals our human wounds by his own (1 Pet. 2:24). . . .

Salvation is the message that our God enfolds our broken reality. A God who embraces us completely—this is God our Savior. Is there a more astonishing miracle in the world than that God embraces our broken reality?[6]

Later he writes: "The church must keep this astonishment alive. The church ceases to exist when she loses this astonishment."[7]

[5] Henri J. M. Nouwen, Donald P. McNeill, and Douglas A. Morrison, *Compassion: A Reflection on the Christian Life* (New York: Doubleday, 1982), 15.
[6] Kazoh Kitamori, *Theology of the Pain of God: The First Original Theology from Japan* (Eugene, OR: Wipf & Stock, 1965), 20.
[7] Ibid., 44.

C. S. Lewis portrays this "astonishing miracle" in one of his *Chronicles of Narnia* books, *The Magician's Nephew*. A young boy named Digory had witnessed Aslan the Lion [the Christ figure in the story] sing Narnia into existence. And because of what he witnessed, Digory began to hope that somehow Aslan would heal his mother back home in London. Aslan had asked Digory to go on a special errand. Digory had agreed . . . I mean, how could he refuse the word of the Lion?

> "Yes," said Digory. He had had for a second some wild idea of saying, "I'll try to help you if you promise to help my Mother," but he realized in time that the Lion was not at all the sort of person one could try to make bargains with. But when he had said "Yes," he thought of his Mother, and he thought of the great hopes he had had, and how they were all dying away, and a lump came in his throat and tears in his eyes, and he blurted out:

> "But please, please—won't you—can't you give something that will cure Mother?" Up till then he had been looking at the Lion's great feet and the huge claws on them; now, in despair, he looked up at its face. What he saw surprised him as much as anything in his whole life. For the tawny face was bent down near his own and (wonder of wonders) great shining tears stood in the Lion's eyes. They were such big, bright tears compared to Digory's

own that for a moment he felt as if the Lion must really be sorrier about his Mother than he was himself.

"My son, my son," said Aslan. "I know. Grief is great."[8]

When you know that the King grieves your grief, you can trust Him to do what is right in the "already, not-yet."

So, in the face of the wreckage, how do we pray? This is what the texts in Matthew lead me to pray:

Lord Jesus,
> You are the great King, and You are the good Shepherd.
> We do not pretend to be able to tell You how to run Your kingdom.
> But because You are the Shepherd-King,
> You invite us to tell You the desire of our hearts.
> And it is this. Will You please . . .

[8] C. S. Lewis, *The Magician's Nephew* (New York: HarperCollins, 1955), 153-154.

2

If You Are Willing

Matthew 8:1-4

¹When Jesus came down from the mountain, large crowds followed Him. ²And a leper came to Him and bowed down before Him, and said, "Lord, if You are willing, You can make me clean." ³Jesus stretched out His hand and touched him, saying, "I am willing; be cleansed." And immediately his leprosy was cleansed. ⁴And Jesus said to him, "See that you tell no one; but go, show yourself to the priest and present the offering that Moses commanded, as a testimony to them."

Preaching, teaching, healing. We saw in the last chapter that this is how Matthew the tax collector summarizes the earthly ministry of Jesus:

Jesus came preaching, announcing the good news of the kingdom.

Jesus came teaching, explaining the good news of the kingdom.

> Jesus came healing, doing the good news of the kingdom.

The kingdom of God is all about redeeming and repairing the broken world. The kingdom is all about restoring and recreating the wrecked world. In His acts of healing, Jesus is making real the news He is announcing and explaining.

PREVENTATIVE MEDICINE

Preaching, teaching, and healing cannot be separated. Indeed, as it turns out, to preach and teach is to heal. Matthew says Jesus goes through villages and towns healing every kind of disease and freeing people from the demonic, and multitudes begin to flock to Him (4:23-25). Understandably so! Then, says Matthew, Jesus goes up on a mountain (5:1). And on the mountain, Jesus preaches and teaches His now famous Sermon on the Mount (chs. 5-7). He begins to teach the relational and ethical dimensions of the gospel of the kingdom.

But it is not as though Jesus suspended His healing work to preach and teach. In preaching and teaching He is continuing to heal. For if we were to actually do what He calls us to do in His Sermon on the Mount, we would experience great healing!

> Deal with your anger, He says.
> Discipline your lust, He says.
> Let go of your desire for revenge, He says.

Love your enemies, He says.

Bless those who persecute you, He says.

Do not let anxiety rule your life, He says.

Forgive as you are forgiven, He says.

Treat people the way you want to be treated,
    He says.

If we actually did what He says to do . . . my, what healing would be unleashed in the world! Jesus's teaching and preaching bring so much healing that we could accurately subtitle His Sermon on the Mount "Preventative Medicine 101."

And then, says Matthew, Jesus goes down the mountain into the valley (8:1). He leaves the mountaintop where He speaks words that heal, and enters into life in the valley where He does deeds that heal.

LEPROSY

The first of Jesus's kingdom deeds is the healing of a man with leprosy. "Jesus stretched out His hand and touched him, saying, 'I am willing; be cleansed'" (v. 3). It would be hard to find a more startling sentence in the first-century context!

This is why Matthew begins the story (in v. 2) with the word "behold," which unfortunately many translations leave out. It is a command: "Look!" Matthew uses this word sixty-two times in his Gospel, and it always conveys astonishment. It is his way of saying, "something unexpected is about to happen." Behold!

Look! Jesus stretched out His hand and touched the man with leprosy. Jesus touched the man!

Of all the diseases of the ancient world, leprosy was the most feared. It was that era's AIDS. Leprosy not only wrecked the body, it also ruined social relationships and (it was thought) destroyed one's spiritual life. People with leprosy were judged to be under a divine curse.

The disease was bad enough. What made matters worse was the way others treated the victims. The historian Josephus tells us that lepers were treated "as if they were in effect, dead persons."[1] They were banished from the community, forced to live outside all walled towns. This meant living outside Jerusalem, the Holy City, which meant away from the temple, which meant being cut off from the worship life of the people of God.

The Old Testament gave a great deal of attention to leprosy because, more than any other form of human brokenness, it symbolized the human condition under the reign of sin. The way leprosy works is a picture of the way sin works. Canon Michael Harper writes:

> Sin separates us from God and from one another. So does leprosy. Sin slowly rots away human life. So does leprosy. Sin is at first not easy to diagnose; it works silently and secretly. So does leprosy. Sin disfigures and distorts. So does leprosy. Sin paralyzes and removes feeling and sensitivity.

---

[1] Josephus, *Antiquities of the Jews* 3.11.3, in *The Works of Josephus*, trans. William Whiston (Lynn, MA: Hendrickson, 1980).

26

So does leprosy. Sin ultimately causes death. So does leprosy.[2]

When King David became aware of the depth of his sin and its consequences, it was the language and imagery of leprosy that he used to describe himself, when he cried out in Psalm 51:7: "Purify me with hyssop, and I shall be clean; Wash me, and I shall be whiter than snow."

Behold! Look! "Jesus stretched out His hand and touched him, saying 'I am willing; be cleansed.' And immediately his leprosy was cleansed." In this one single act we see the transforming nature of the kingdom of God, and we have a sign of the full-orbed holistic salvation Jesus came to bring.

I invite you to look at this astonishing event in three stages. First, let us take a careful look at how Jesus relates to the man with leprosy. Second, let us then take a look at how the man relates to Jesus. Third, let us wrestle with the tough questions the event raises.

HOW JESUS RELATES TO THE MAN

First, look at how Jesus relates to the man. Notice the two attributes of Jesus's character at work here: His authority and His compassion.

His authority. Jesus speaks. No weird incantations, no waving of a magic wand, no chanting of a secret mantra, no fanfare, no hype. Just "Be cleansed." There

[2] Michael Harper, *The Healings of Jesus* (Downers Grove: InterVarsity, 1986), 63.

was no appeal to any higher authority; Jesus does not pray or invoke the power of God. He just speaks: "Be cleansed." Who is this who simply by speaking makes things happen? Who is this who speaks, and what He speaks comes into being?

And compassion. Jesus touches the man! No one in that day touched people who had leprosy. You think people are afraid to touch AIDS patients; that fear pales before the first-century fear of leprosy victims. William Barclay explains:

> If a leper so much as put his head into a house, that house became unclean even to the roof beams. . . . No one might come nearer to a leper than four cubits [6 feet]. . . . If the wind was blowing towards a person from a leper the leper must stand at least 100 cubits [150 feet] away. One Rabbi would not even eat an egg bought in a street where a leper had passed by.[3]

"Jesus stretched out His hand and touched the man." The word Matthew uses (*haptomia*) actually means "to attach oneself to." Jesus attached Himself to the man! Jesus broke through all the hygienic uptightness, and through all the fear, and grasped the diseased man. Jesus risked His own health and He risked being ostracized, for according to "the rules" He was now technically unclean.

[3] William Barclay, *The Gospel of Matthew: Volume 1 (Chapters 1-10)*, rev. ed. (Philadelphia: Westminster, 1975), 296.

He touched. The gospel is in that one little verb, is it not? The Holy One attaches Himself to the unholy!

Linger here a moment. Let this picture of Jesus touching the "uncleanest of the unclean" fill your imagination. It seems to me that most believers live with a very different picture. We visualize Jesus approaching the man and keeping a polite, safe distance. Jesus says to the man, "Go over there to that bathtub, wash yourself real good, and you will be clean." The man obeys, washes, and comes out clean. In joy He returns to Jesus. And then Jesus touches him—after the cleaning.

Most of us feel that Jesus only attaches Himself to us after we are clean. We therefore spend all kinds of spiritual energy trying to get ourselves to a place where we are acceptable to Him. But Jesus touches the unclean man *before* He speaks the cleansing word! Compassion: the Holy One grabs hold of us before He makes us holy!

Note a further act of compassion in this story. Jesus tells the man to go show himself to the priests and offer the gift Moses commands for such cases. Because people were so fearful about leprosy, provision was made for the unlikely event of a cure. A person had to go through an elaborate ritual (see Lev. 14). Afterward, the person was thoroughly examined and then given a certificate stating that he or she was healed enough not to infect others. The certificate would alleviate others' fears. No more would he have to stay outside. No more would she have to yell, "Unclean! Unclean!" By saying "Go, show yourself to the priest," Jesus heals the social dimensions of brokenness. Jesus attached Himself to the man, and then does everything He can to get the man attached to his community.

On that particular day, authority and compassion came together in Jesus's great declaration, "I am willing." Authority and compassion merge into the will to make a human being whole. On that day, Jesus's authority and compassion came together to announce the gospel: "I am willing to make you whole."

His name, after all, is Jesus, Yeshua: Yahweh saves, Yahweh-to-the-rescue. His crucifixion demonstrates how far He is willing to go to fulfill His name. And His resurrection demonstrates how able He is to do what His name means.

HOW THE MAN RELATES TO JESUS

Look now at how the man relates to Jesus. I am amazed at the man's grasp of the compassion of Jesus. Somehow this man knew Jesus would not reject him. Amazing! How many times had he seen people turn on their heels and run from him? How many times had he heard the pious folk yell, "You stay away"? How many times had people thrown rocks at him to keep him at bay? Constant rejection usually hardens us. What was it that freed the man to see in Jesus one who would not turn His back?

I am also amazed at the man's grasp of the authority of Jesus. The great preacher of the fourth century John Chrysostom calls us to admire the man's "right opinion" about Jesus.[4] The man did not say to Jesus, "If you request it of God, I can be clean." He said to Jesus, "If You are willing, You can make me clean." How did he know this?

In the way the man relates to Jesus we find a model of the kind of faith that participates in the gospel of the kingdom. Call it bold humility or humble boldness; eager reverence or reverent eagerness: "If You are willing, You are able."

Many suggest that the "if" is due to all the rejection this man had experienced, and reflects a poor self-image. It is said that the "if" expresses the man's doubt whether Jesus cares. I disagree. If the man was crippled by a poor self-image, or if he doubted Jesus cared, he would not have broken all the rules to get close enough to kneel before Jesus.

I think the man's "if you are willing" is due to his recognition of who Jesus is. "Lord," says the man. No one tells the Lord what to do! "If you are willing" is the word of a human being who recognizes his or her place before the Lord. Dale Bruner puts it this way:

> Faith does not demand help as a right; it is modest and respectful, and, while bold enough [to come] . . . faith still keeps its place . . . and bows before the sovereign pleasure of the one it calls Lord.[5]

[4] Quoted in F. Dale Bruner, *The Christbook: A Historical/Theological Commentary, Matthew 1-12* (Waco: Word Books, 1987), 300.
[5] Ibid., 299.

To pray, "Lord, if it be Your will" is reverence. By the blood of the Lamb we may boldly approach the throne of grace (Heb. 4:16), but it is still a throne. "If you want to" is the language of a heart aware of its place before the Holy One.

"If You are willing, You can make me clean." Faith does not demand. But faith is sure the Lord can meet the need. Do we know that? Do we believe Jesus is able? Do we believe He can do the humanly impossible? Where did the man get that confidence? Dale Bruner rightly proclaims that "this fine combination of modesty ('if you want to') and confidence ('you can') is true faith."[6]

IS HE WILLING?

We come then to the questions this event raises. Jesus says to the plea of the man with leprosy, "I am willing; be cleansed." The main question we have is whether Jesus is always willing. I once saw on a pastor's bulletin board the saying, "You never have to ask, 'Is it God's will to heal?'" I agree . . . in the larger scheme of things. In the cross and in the empty tomb God has revealed His great passion to make us whole.

It is God's will to one day rid the whole world of sin. It is God's will to one day completely heal creation. But before that day, can we say so boldly, "You never have to ask, 'Is it God's will to heal?'"

I know that Jesus never rejects anyone who comes to

[6] Ibid.

Him in and with their brokenness. I know that in Jesus I have met someone who feels my brokenness, who has the ability to put me together again and who wants to make me like Himself, holy and whole. I have witnessed Him touching many people and restoring them to health. He has done so for me many times!

But what of those times we do not receive the specific healing we requested? Does that mean He was unwilling? There are no easy, one-size-fits-all answers. The kingdom is, after all, "already, not-yet." "I am willing." Definitively so in the larger picture. What about right now, today?

I do know that in a broken world some pain can be a good gift, as is seen in what is sometimes called "redemptive suffering." In some cases, Jesus allows the pain because it calls out to us, "Something is wrong and you are not paying attention . . . and I am not going away until you do."

Many know the name of Paul Brand, a doctor who for years worked in India with people who suffered with leprosy. Dr. Brand argues that the worst thing about the disease is the inability to feel pain. People lose their fingers and toes not because of something organically wrong with the digits, but because of the loss of sensation. When, for instance, they step on a nail, they do not feel any pain. Dr. Brand says: "If I could choose one gift for leprosy patients it would be the gift of pain."[7] So some pain is good, redemptive.

[7] Paul Brand with Philip Yancey, "And God Created Pain," *Christianity*

Yet I also know that Jesus finds no delight in anyone's pain. And I know that He will not be satisfied until we are completely restored.

So . . . recognizing that there are no easy answers, let me ask some different questions. I am in no way suggesting that doing so will solve the mystery. But I do think they will help us get at some of the deeper issues involved. And in the process, they will help us cooperate more fully with Jesus the Healer.

ARE WE BRINGING BROKENNESS TO JESUS?

Question one: Are we, like the man with leprosy, bringing our brokenness to Jesus? We can say all the right words, but in reality we may only be moaning and groaning, never really intending to give Jesus any of it. We can call out His name, but not really be calling upon Him. Not every "Praise the Lord" is actually meant for the Lord's ears, and not every "O God!" is actually aimed at God.

Helmut Thielicke, the great German preacher-theologian, suggested that much of what we call prayer is really nothing more than a "primal scream." An elderly man is high on a stepladder cleaning the rain gutters. The ladder begins to slide on the ground, and, as he falls, he cries out, "O mother!" Is he calling his mother? No. Are we in fact praying when we pray? Are we in fact bringing ourselves to Jesus?

Today 38, no. 1 (January 10, 1994), 20.

Here we can take a clue from the man with leprosy. Matthew says he came to Jesus and "bowed down" (8:2). The word (*proskuneo*) is translated elsewhere as "worship." The man came and worshipped Jesus. *Proskuneo* literally means "to come forward and kiss." Would it be right to say that when we are in fact bringing our need to Jesus there is the note of tender reverence?

But even then we can miss the point. For not all that we call "worship" is actually authentically God-directed. It is so easy to be seeking what "worship" does for us more than actually seeking the One to be worshipped. So are we in fact bringing our brokenness to Jesus?

DO WE WANT TO GET WELL?

Question two: Are we in fact willing to be healed, to be cleansed? Do we really want what He can give us? Forgive me if this feels like I am harsh, putting the blame on us for not being healed. But I know from personal experience that there are times when I do not want to let go of certain forms of brokenness. As bad as they might be, at least they are familiar. Deeper still, the brokenness has become part of my identity. I would not know how to function apart from it.

As we noted in the last chapter, Jesus asked a man who had been lame for decades, "Do you wish to get well?" (John 5:6). Of course he does! Or does he? If Jesus makes his legs well, the man's life will change—dramatically so! He will have to accept more responsibility for his own welfare. He will no longer have an excuse on those days when he mistreats the people around him. The dynamics of all his relationships will change!

This is why doctors and other health care workers ask us the kinds of questions they ask. Before choosing a specific treatment plan, they ask us questions to find out our attitude toward ourselves and the presenting sickness, questions like the following:[8]

"Do you want to live to be a hundred?"
Whoa . . . that one raises all kinds of issues!
"What happened to you in the year or two before your illness?"
That was a very helpful one for me after I had a heart attack in August 2012.

"What does the illness mean to you?"
Does this illness somehow define us?
Does it give us a sense of identity in the world?
And the big question: "Why do you need this illness?"
This one sounds cruel, I know. I remember the first time I was asked it!

You see, sickness gives us "permission" not to do things we do not want to do, or to do things we would otherwise feel afraid to do. We are so complex that even when presented with a way to healing, we are not sure to act on it.

---

[8] I first discovered these questions in Bernie S. Siegel, *Love, Medicine and Miracles* (New York: HarperCollins, 1986), 105-112. While I do not endorse everything in this book, I have found these questions helpful.

In *Change or Die* Alan Deutschman poses this question:

> Change or die. What if you were given that choice? . . . What if a well-informed, trusted authority figure said you had to make difficult and enduring changes in the way you think, feel, and act. If you didn't, your time would end soon—a lot sooner than it had to. Could you change when changes really mattered? When it mattered most?[9]

Deutschman worked with hundreds of people—politicians, CEOs, professors, doctors—who had a life-threatening issue, like a heart attack or cancer, and who were told they had to make major changes if they wanted to live longer. Only ten percent of the people he worked with made the changes.

I remembered this book on the evening I was told I was having a heart attack, and I vowed that I would make whatever changes I had to in order to live the life Jesus is calling me to live. I vowed I would be the ten percent. It has not been easy. Eating well and running at the gym has been relatively straightforward. But the Lord has shown me, more clearly than before, that there are more fundamental changes I need to make. And those changes are coming more slowly. But if I want to be all Jesus wants me to be—for Him, for my wife,

[9] Alan Deutschman, *Change or Die: The Three Keys to Change at Work and in Life* (New York: HarperCollins, 2007), 1.

Sharon, for my family, for the church, for the kingdom—I have to keep embracing His call to change.

DO WE WANT THE FULL TREATMENT?

Jesus's willingness to heal goes beyond any particular problem. Jesus comes to cure the whole of us. Do we want what He is prepared to give?

Notice that in the story neither the man nor Jesus use the verb "heal." That is what happens, but it is not the word used to describe what happens. Rather, both use the word "cleanse." "If You are willing, You can make me clean." "I am willing; be cleansed."

As I mentioned earlier, leprosy symbolizes the greater disease that needs the greater cure. "Cleanse" refers to the deeper, higher, wider work Jesus comes to do. Jesus comes not just to cure but to change, to make us more like Himself. Do we want what He is prepared to do?

Here I quote an insight of C.S. Lewis found in *Mere Christianity*:

> When I was a child I often had a toothache, and I knew that if I went to my mother she would give me something which would deaden the pain for the night and let me get to sleep. But I did not go to my mother—at least, not till the pain became very bad. And the reason I did not go was this. I did not doubt she would give me the aspirin; but I knew she would also do something else. I knew she would take me to the dentist next morning. I could not get what I wanted out of

her without getting something more, which I did not want. I wanted immediate relief from pain: but I could not get it without having my teeth set permanently right. And I knew those dentists; I knew they started fiddling about with all sorts of other teeth which had not yet begun to ache. They would not let sleeping dogs lie; if you gave them an inch they took an ell.

Now, if I may put it that way, Our Lord is like the dentists. If you give Him an inch, He will take an ell. Dozens of people go to Him to be cured of some one particular sin which they are ashamed of (like masturbation or physical cowardice) or which is obviously spoiling daily life (like bad temper or drunkenness). Well, He will cure it all right: but He will not stop there. That may be all you asked; but if once you call Him in, He will give you the full treatment.

That is why he warned people to "count the cost" before becoming Christians. "Make no mistake," He says, "if you let me, I will make you perfect. The moment you put yourself in My hands, that is what you are in for. Nothing less, or other, than that. You have free will, and if you choose, you can push Me away. But if you do not push Me away, understand that I am going to see the job through. Whatever suffering it may cost you in your earthly life, whatever inconceivable purification it may cost you after death, whatever it

costs Me, I will never rest, nor let you rest, until
you are literally perfect—until my Father can say
without reservation that He is well pleased with
you, as He said He was well pleased with me.
This I can do and will do. But I will not do anything less."[10]

Do we want the full treatment? Are we willing to go for
radical surgery?

Jesus came preaching, teaching, and healing. And
Behold! Look! Jesus stretched out His hand and
touched the man with leprosy. The time is fulfilled; the
kingdom of God has come near. In Jesus, the Living
God has revealed His passion to make us whole. In
Jesus, the Living God is moving history toward that
day when you and I and the whole created order will
receive the final cure.

So, what do we do today? I think we should do
what the man with leprosy did. He did not know all
the answers. He did not know what would happen in
bringing himself before Jesus. But somehow he knew
that Jesus would not turn him away. Somehow he knew
that Jesus would meet him in his need. So he came,
and threw himself on Jesus's authority and compassion.
"Lord, if You want to You can make me clean." Let us
do the same. "Lord, here I am. Here is where I need
You to work in me. If You want to, You can do it."

[10] C. S. Lewis, *Mere Christianity* (New York: Macmillan, 1952), 171-172.

3

Just Say the Word

Matthew 8:5-13

5And when Jesus entered Capernaum, a centurion came to Him, imploring Him, 6and saying, "Lord, my servant is lying paralyzed at home, fearfully tormented." 7Jesus said to him, "I will come and heal him." 8But the centurion said, "Lord, I am not worthy for You to come under my roof, but just say the word, and my servant will be healed. 9For I also am a man under authority, with soldiers under me; and I say to this one, 'Go!' and he goes, and to another, 'Come!' and he comes, and to my slave, 'Do this!' and he does it." 10Now when Jesus heard this, He marveled and said to those who were following, "Truly I say to you, I have not found such great faith with anyone in Israel. 11I say to you that many will come from east and west, and recline at the table with Abraham, Isaac and Jacob in the kingdom of heaven; 12but the sons of the kingdom will be cast out into the outer darkness; in that place there will be weeping and gnashing of teeth." ¹³And Jesus said to the centurion, "Go; it shall be done for you as you have believed." And the servant was healed that very moment.

On only two occasions do we find the statement "Jesus marveled." There may have been others, but the Gospels record only two times when Jesus was astonished.

One was in Jesus's hometown, in Nazareth. People who had known Him all His life were offended at what Jesus was saying and doing. Mark tells us, "He [Jesus] could do no miracle there except that He laid His hands on a few sick people and healed them. And He wondered at their unbelief" (Mark 6:5-6).

The other occasion is the one before us in this passage. It took place in Capernaum, a town on the north shore of the Sea of Galilee, where Jesus had made His headquarters during the early period of His ministry. A Gentile, that is, a person who is not expected to have faith, comes to Jesus, and Matthew tells us that Jesus marveled. He turned to those who were following Him and said, "Truly I say to you, I have not found such great faith with anyone in Israel" (8:10).

If Jesus was amazed, think of what those around Him must have felt! A Roman centurion, a foreign soldier in charge of a hundred other foreign soldiers, a man who came from a pagan home, who had no formal religious training . . . exercises faith greater than those who had all the benefits of synagogue services and teachers. A man who is not expected to see does, while those who think they see do not.

Before exploring the centurion's "great faith," I want to note something else which no doubt amazed the people that day. The centurion came to Jesus on behalf of a servant, grieved that a servant was suffering. This is amazing, because in the Roman Empire, servants simply did not matter. Aristotle, for example, writes:

There can be no friendship nor justice towards inanimate things; indeed, not even towards a horse or an ox, nor yet towards a slave as a slave. For master and slave have nothing in common; a slave is a living tool, just as a tool is an inanimate slave.[1]

A slave had no rights—legal or otherwise. As far as most masters were concerned, "the only difference between a slave and a beast or a cart was that the slave could speak."[2] In that value system, disabled servants especially had no value.

Yet this centurion goes out of his way to get help for his servant who is paralyzed. He does the unexpected, and in many people's minds, the unnecessary. Is the state of his heart, as manifested in his attitude toward

[1] Quoted by William Barclay, *The Gospel of Matthew: Volume 1 (Chapters 1-10)*, rev. ed. (Philadelphia: Westminster, 1975), 302.
[2] Ibid.

servants, part of the reason the centurion can exercise the faith Jesus calls "great"? Is the centurion's care for his servant a sign that the kingdom of heaven has come near to him?

The rest of the New Testament certainly makes this point. How we are relating to other people says something about how we are relating to the Living God. How we relate to servants says volumes.

Let us now try to get inside the "great faith" of the centurion. I am amazed at the man's grasp of Jesus's compassion and at his grasp of Jesus's authority. Consider each separately.

FAITH IN JESUS'S COMPASSION

Notice that the man feels no need to beg Jesus for help. He feels no need to go into great detail about the problem. He simply states the need: "Lord, my servant is lying paralyzed at home, fearfully tormented" (8:6).

Here we have a very liberating lesson on prayer. As G. Campbell-Morgan of England puts it, "All the prayers that storm heaven are brief."[3] The centurion simply stated the need. His faith was in Jesus's compassion, not in his own ability to articulate the need. How did the man know that? How did he know that all he needed to do was say, "Lord, my servant is not well"?

---

[3] G. Campbell Morgan, *Studies in the Four Gospels* (Old Tappen, NJ: Fleming H. Revell), 84.

And how did he know that Jesus would not refuse him? Matthew says, "When Jesus entered Capernaum, a centurion came to Him" (8:5). In order to "come to Jesus," the centurion had to break through all kinds of racial, cultural, and spiritual barriers. How did he know Jesus would let him through?

There was no higher or thicker barrier in the first century than that between Jew and Gentile. For many Jews of that day, the only appropriate word for a Gentile was "dog." Gentiles were "outsiders." At the great kingdom banquet at the end of history, Gentiles might be present, but only as servants.

Yet this Gentile dares to approach Jesus the Jew and express a need. How did he know he would not be refused? I mean, look at the strikes against the guy. He was a Gentile. And he was no ordinary Gentile, but one working for the foreign power dominating the Jews. And Rome was no ordinary power, for Rome was exploiting and oppressing Israel. What made this Gentile enemy feel he could come to Jesus and not be rejected? Amazing! He just comes and throws himself on the compassion of Jesus.

And he is not disappointed. For Jesus immediately responds, "I will come and heal him" (8:7). Amazing grace! Jesus will go to the centurion's house. It was shocking for Jesus to reach out and touch a leper. It was even more shocking that he would be willing to go into the house of a Gentile. The religious law of the day laid it down that houses of Gentiles were spiritually contaminated. In the Mishnah it says, "The dwelling places of Gentiles are unclean."[4]

The centurion had banked on Jesus's compassion, but he was not ready for that much!

FAITH IN JESUS'S AUTHORITY

Consider now the man's grasp of Jesus's authority. The centurion expresses his shock to Jesus's surprise declaration by saying, "Lord, I am not worthy for You to come under my roof" (8:8). And then he goes on to say that even if he were worthy there is no need for Jesus to come to his house: "Just say the word, and my servant will be healed" (8:8).

It is this that impresses and astonishes Jesus. It is this that Jesus calls "great faith." Great faith is confidence that all Jesus need do is speak.

The centurion reasons from his own experience. As a soldier he is under authority and exercises authority over others. He says to one of his soldiers "go," and he goes. He says to another "come," and he comes. He says to a servant "do this," and he does it.

Somehow the centurion recognized that the compassionate One need only say "Be healed," and it would happen. Just as the centurion has authority over a hundred troops, so Jesus has authority over life and death. When the centurion speaks to his soldiers, he is obeyed, and he realizes that Jesus can likewise "give

[4] Barclay, *Matthew*, 303.

orders affecting the welfare of human beings which would be instantly obeyed, whether He was in their presence or not."[5]

How did the centurion know this? How did he know that Jesus Christ has that kind of authority? He came and threw himself on that authority, and was not disappointed. Jesus spoke, and the servant (who is nowhere near the place where Jesus and the centurion are talking) was made whole. The servant was made whole by a person he does not see, who speaks a word he does not hear.

THE PERFORMATIVE WORD

It seems to me that one of the greatest needs of the church today is to recover confidence in the word of Jesus Christ. Jesus need only speak, and something happens.

We all know the power of our words. One word can change the atmosphere of a room. Yell "fire!" in a crowded theatre, and watch what happens. Or hear a pastor say, "I now pronounce you husband and wife." Things change!

If our words have such power, think of the word of Jesus Christ, the Divine Word made flesh (John 1:14). His word not only informs, it performs. His word not only announces, it accomplishes what He announces.

"Be clean," and the leper is made whole.

[5] R.G.V. Tasker, *The Gospel According to St. Matthew: An Introduction and Commentary* (Grand Rapids: Wm. B. Eerdmans, 1961), 88.

"Be still," and the sea is calm.
"Be gone," and the demons flee.
"Lazarus, come forth," and the dead man walks
    out of the tomb.

I believe Matthew intends for us to hear in Jesus's word an echo of the original creative word, an echo of that moment when into the darkness and chaos of nothingness there came "Let there be light" . . . and there was. Jesus's word is the word of the Creator come into all the mess, the word that accomplishes what it announces.

This is why we can put all our weight on His promises. What He speaks will come into being. Remember Jesus's first word to Simon the fisherman? "'You are Simon the son of John; you shall be called Cephas' (which is translated Peter)" (John 1:42). You are shifting sand, and shall be called Rock. And it happened.

Remember Jesus's word to the early church? "You will receive power when the Holy Spirit has come upon you; and you shall be My witnesses both in Jerusalem, and in all Judea and Samaria, and even to the remotest part of the earth" (Acts 1:8). And it happened. What Jesus speaks comes into being.

This is also how we are to understand His commandments. Most of us read the Law, the Ten Commandments, this way:

I am Yahweh your God, who took you out of
    the house of slavery.
Now get on with it and

have no other gods before Me,
keep the Sabbath,
do not murder,
do not covet, and so on.

But that is because we fail to grasp the performative nature of His word.

This is how we are to read the commandments:
I am Yahweh your God, who took you out of
    the house of slavery.
You *will* have no other gods before Me.
You *will* keep the Sabbath.
You *will* not murder.
You *will* not covet, and so on.

The Word empowers the obedience it commands.

"You shall be holy, for I the LORD your God am holy" (Lev. 19:2). Most of us read it this way: "I am holy, therefore get with it and behave like Me!" No, no, no. His word brings into being what it commands. "You will be holy . . . just like Me."

Jesus says in the Sermon on the Mount, "You are to be perfect, as your heavenly Father is perfect." (Matt. 5:48). Most of us read it this way: "Here is your task: work at being like the Father." No! His word brings into being what it commands: "You will be perfect." What he speaks will come into being.

"Just say the word," because if You do Lord, something happens.

HEARING THE WORD

So, where do we hear this word? How does it come to us? In many places, and in many ways (Heb. 1:1). But primarily it comes to us in and through the Bible, the written word of the Lord. The degree of spiritual, mental, emotional, and physical "aliveness" that we have is directly related to how much we live in the pages of the Bible. When we live in those pages, we are exposing ourselves to the performative word of the Creator and Redeemer.

Do you want to live? Take the Book off the shelf and read it! You say it does not work anymore? Nothing happens? Then try reading it out loud. Read one of the Gospels out loud, or read Isaiah 40-66 out loud, or read Revelation out loud, and see if you can sit still. You will be dancing with life!

John White, a Canadian psychiatrist, argues that one of the ways to help overcome depression is to engage in solid, inductive Bible study—to go beyond mere devotional reading. He writes:

> Years ago, when I was seriously depressed, the thing that saved my own sanity was a dry-as-dust grappling with Hosea's prophecy. I spent weeks, morning by morning, making meticulous notes, checking historical allusions in the text. Slowly I began to sense the ground under my feet growing steadily firmer. I knew without any doubt that healing was constantly springing

from my struggle to grasp the meaning of the prophecy.[6]

This is because the word of the Living Lord accomplishes what it announces.

Just ask Matthew. One day he was sitting in his tax office. Jesus walked by, looked at Matthew, and said, "Follow Me!" (Matt. 9:9). And Matthew got up and followed. He had to—the word Jesus speaks brings into being what He speaks. When you hear that word, you cannot but obey.

"Just say the word." How did the centurion know that healing happens through the performative word of Jesus? "I will come to your house," says Jesus. "No, You don't need to come. Just speak the word." And Jesus marveled, saying, "I have never found such great faith."

I invite you to be still for a while and in the stillness, bring your need to the One who is closer than your breathing and say: "Just say the word Lord, for if You do, something happens."

[6] John White, *The Masks of Melancholy: A Christian Physician Looks at Depression and Suicide* (Downers Grove: InterVarsity, 1982), 202-203.

4

He Takes and Carries

Matthew 8:14-17

14When Jesus came into Peter's home, He saw his mother-in-law lying sick in bed with a fever. 15He touched her hand, and the fever left her; and she got up and waited on Him.

16When evening came, they brought to Him many who were demon-possessed; and He cast out the spirits with a word, and healed all who were ill. 17This was to fulfill what was spoken through Isaiah the prophet:

"He Himself took our infirmities and carried away our diseases."

The central point of Matthew 8:14-17 is sounded in the last line, in Matthew's theological interpretation of the healing deeds of Jesus: "This was to fulfill what was spoken through Isaiah the prophet: 'He Himself took our infirmities and carried away our diseases.'"

In chapters 8 and 9 of his Gospel, Matthew the tax collector has gathered up ten of the many "mighty deeds" Jesus performed during the early stages of His earthly ministry. Jesus performed a whole lot more! The ten "mighty deeds" manifest "the gospel of the kingdom," the good news Jesus came preaching and teaching.

In the text we will be looking at in this chapter, we have the third of the ten deeds.

The first is the healing of the man with leprosy. Jesus stretches out His hand and touches the man, saying, "I am willing; be cleansed," and the leprosy left him (8:3).

The second is the healing of a centurion's servant. The Roman soldier entreats Jesus to do something for his servant who lies at home, paralyzed, suffering great pain (8:5-6). Jesus tells the soldier, "Go; it shall be done for you as you have believed," and the servant was healed that very moment (8:13).

And the third is the healing of Simon Peter's mother-in-law. Jesus comes into Peter's home, sees the woman sick in bed with a fever, touches her hand, and the fever leaves her (8:15).

Then Matthew says that Jesus does these three (and all His other acts of healing) "to fulfill what was spoken through Isaiah the prophet: 'He Himself took our infirmities and carried away our diseases.'" What is

Matthew getting at in his interpretation? What does he want us to know about Jesus? And what are the implications for us today?

Before we give our attention to Matthew's insight, let me hold before us a number of other themes at work in this third healing event. Each theme is worthy of a separate chapter!

JESUS'S COMPASSION FOR THE OUTSIDER

The first theme is Jesus's compassion for the outsider. In the first century, women were treated as second-class citizens. Actually, they were not treated as "citizens" at all! They had no rights, legal or otherwise. They were thought to be "possessions," property of men. If single, a woman was the property of her father; if married, she was the property of her husband. In the series of prayers males were to pray every morning, Jewish men thanked God that they were not born a Gentile, a slave, or a woman![1]

There were all kinds of rules regulating women's relationships with men. Two particularly help us appreciate what Jesus is doing in the healing of Peter's mother-in-law. One, a man was never to touch a woman's hand. This was all part of a larger ban on touching things "unclean." And two, a man was not to be waited on by a woman. She could cook the meal and clean

[1] William Barclay, *The Letters to Timothy, Titus, and Philemon*, rev. ed. (Philadelphia: Westminster, 1975), 67.

up afterwards, but she was not to wait on a man, lest, as one rabbi put it, she "become accustomed to being around men."[2]

Do you see the radical thing Jesus the Healer is doing? "When Jesus had come into Peter's house, He saw Peter's mother-in-law lying in bed with a fever." And what does He do? "He touched her hand!" She had a fever. You would think He would touch her head first. But no, He touches her hand. Breaking the rules, bringing healing at many levels.

And, when the fever left her, "she got up and began to wait on" Jesus. And He does not correct her! Jesus lets a woman wait on Him! Jesus wants women to become accustomed to being around men! This is the kingdom of heaven breaking into human society! In the kingdom Jesus is bringing into the world, women are not second-class citizens. Women are welcomed into the great fellowship as equal partakers of grace.

In Matthew's Gospel, Jesus is always breaking down the barriers that divide. He reaches out and touches a leper. He talks to a Gentile soldier. And He touches a woman's hand. Jesus has compassion for the outsider.

SIMPLY BY TOUCH

The second theme I want to draw to your attention is that Jesus restores simply by touch.

---

[2] F. Dale Bruner, *The Christbook: A Historical/Theological Commentary, Matthew 1-12* (Waco: Word Books, 1987), 308.

In the healing of the leper,
    He heals by both touch and speech.
In the healing of the centurion's servant,
    He heals simply by speech.
In the healing of Peter's mother-in-law,
    He heals simply by touch.

Jesus heals by speaking: His authority. And by touching: His compassion.

I wonder if this is not why we have two creation accounts in the Bible. In Genesis 1, God creates by speaking. We hear "and God said" ten times. Then in Genesis 2, God creates by touching. "Then the LORD God formed man of dust from the ground, and breathed into his nostrils the breath of life" (2:7). God acts as a potter, intimately involved with the clay, handling it, shaping it. Even more! God then kisses the lifeless clay into true humanity. Jesus creates by speaking and touching. And Jesus heals by speaking and touching.

This is why throughout the centuries, the church has emphasized both Word and Table. We need to hear the Word, the Voice of God. We do not live by bread alone, but by every word that proceeds from the mouth of God. And we need to feel His hand at the Table, where He offers us bread and wine, touching our bodies.

THE SOVEREIGN FREEDOM OF JESUS

The third theme is the sovereign freedom of Jesus. Did you notice as we read the text that no one asks Jesus to act? Jesus is not responding to any spoken prayer. He is acting in unsolicited grace! He heals simply because He chooses to heal.

In the first of the ten deeds, the man with leprosy asks for help: "If You are willing, You can make me clean." In the second of the ten deeds, the Roman soldier asks for help: "Just say the word, and my servant will be healed." But in the third of the ten deeds, no one cries out for help.

This puts the whole matter of divine healing in a larger perspective. Yes, Jesus heals in response to faith-filled praying. But at rock bottom, Jesus acts to heal because He wants to heal. How many of us are as well as we are, not because we asked Him to work in us, but because He simply chose to work in us?

Jesus sees Peter's mother-in-law lying there. And without being asked, He touches her hand. The sovereign freedom of Jesus reminds us that in the final analysis, God's work in the world is not determined by how much we ask Him to work!

SERVICE IS THE FRUIT OF HEALING

One more theme is at work in the story: service is the fruit of healing, not the price paid to get healed. Peter's mother-in-law waits on Jesus not to get grace, but because grace has gotten her. Her serving flows out of grace. Serving done to get grace is grace-less. It is touchy, possessive, and usually minimalist. Serving done out of being gotten by grace is grace-full. It radiates gratitude and joy; it is warm and extravagant.

INTERPRETATION

Okay. Let us now focus on the heart of the text, on Matthew's theological interpretation of Jesus's acts of healing. Matthew sees Jesus's healing ministry as the fulfillment of promise. He claims that Jesus's deeds fulfill the prophecy spoken through Isaiah: "He Himself took our infirmities and carried away our diseases" (8:17). Jesus took and carried our sickness.

Matthew heard this prophecy in chapter 53 in the massive work of Isaiah.[3] Isaiah 53 is the fourth of the so-called "Servant of Yahweh Songs" in Isaiah. In it the prophet paints a picture of someone who comes and suffers on behalf of sinful humanity. The New Testament says the someone is Jesus of Nazareth; the Servant of Isaiah 53 is Jesus. So much so, that many refer to Isaiah 53 as the "fifth gospel": Matthew, Mark, Luke, John, and Isaiah 53. Matthew is saying that in His acts of healing, Jesus is living out the prophecy of Isaiah 53.

Now, many people are puzzled by Matthew's use of Isaiah 53 relative to Jesus's healing ministry. That is, many are surprised by Matthew referring to Isaiah 53 before Jesus is crucified, for it is thought that Isaiah 53 speaks only of Jesus's suffering on the cross. John Calvin, one of the great reformers of the sixteenth century, was troubled by Matthew's use of Isaiah 53:

This oracle seems awkwardly cited, if not twisted

---

[3] More specifically, in Isaiah 52:13-53:12. In this chapter, when I refer to Isaiah 53, I am referring to this wider text.

into another meaning, for Isaiah spoke there not of miracles, but of Christ's death, not of temporal benefits, but of spiritual and eternal grace.[4]

"Awkwardly cited," "twisted into another meaning." Is Calvin right? Has Matthew twisted the meaning of Isaiah 53?

Spiritualizing Sickness

The only way to decide is to go back and listen to Isaiah carefully. When we do, we discover that the healing of sickness is a major thread in the Servant of Yahweh song. Eight times in the song Isaiah uses words that refer to real, physical sickness. Yet, most translations "spiritualize" the words. They render the words as "sorrow" or "grief," or the general word "suffering."

Isaiah 53:3 is a familiar line if you have been in the church long: "He [the Servant] was despised and forsaken of men, a man of sorrows and acquainted with grief." The word rendered "sorrows" (*mak'ob*) literally means "pain," real physical pain. The word rendered "grief" (*holi*) literally means "sickness," real physical sickness. Isaiah sees in the coming Servant "a man of pains, acquainted with sickness."

Isaiah 53:4 is the text Matthew cites, and it is usually rendered, "Surely our griefs He Himself bore, and our sorrows He carried." When Matthew quotes it he reads

---

[4] John Calvin, *Calvin's Commentaries: A Harmony of the Gospels Matthew, Mark, and Luke*, trans. A. W. Morrison (Grand Rapids: Eerdmans, 1972), 1:163.

"infirmities" not "griefs," and "diseases" not "sorrows." Has he changed the text of Isaiah?

No. The word rendered "sorrows" in verse 4 is the same word rendered as "sorrows" in verse 3, and it means "pains," the pains of sickness. Isaiah sees in the coming Servant, one who takes up our sickness and carries our pains.

In his book, *God So Loved the Third World,* Thomas Hanks points out that this sickness thread is so strong in the song that Isaiah uses words and images associated with leprosy to describe the Servant. The word usually translated "stricken" in 53:4, and "to whom the stroke was due" in 53:8 (one a verb, *naga*, the other a noun, *nega*) occurs seventy times in the Old Testament, fifty-four times in Leviticus 13 and 14 where it explicitly refers to leprosy.[5]

The way Isaiah describes the people's reaction to the Servant suggests he suffers some sort of leprosy-like illness. Isaiah 52:14 says that "His appearance was marred more than any man and His form more than the sons of men," or, as the NIV has it, "and his form marred beyond human likeness." Isaiah 53:3 says that "like one from whom men [and women] hide their face, He was despised."

Isaiah is not saying that the Servant of the Lord contracts leprosy. But he is suggesting that the Servant

---

[5] Thomas D. Hanks, *God So Loved the Third World: The Biblical Vocabulary of Oppression* (Eugene, OR: Wipf & Stock, 1984), 76-77.

suffers some sort of similar disfiguring sickness. Thus, some older versions of the Bible render 53:4 ("We ourselves esteemed Him stricken, smitten of God, and afflicted") as "We considered Him a leper, wounded and humiliated by God."[6]

There's more! "But the LORD was pleased to crush Him, putting Him to grief" (Isa. 53:10). The verb translated "putting Him to grief" literally means "to make sick" (*heheli*). Isaiah sees in the coming Servant, one whom the Lord makes sick.

Why? Why would this happen? Isaiah 53:5: "and by His scourging we are healed." "Scourging" is literally "wounds" or "bruises." By His wounds we are *rapha'*, made whole.

No wonder Isaiah exclaims near the beginning of the Servant Song: "Who has believed our message?" (Isa. 53:1).

The Servant of the Lord comes to restore God's people by taking up their sickness to the degree He Himself is made sick? He heals our wounds by being wounded Himself?

I think you can see now that Matthew has not twisted the message of Isaiah 53. Not to worry John Calvin, Matthew quotes Isaiah accurately. The tax collector-evangelist sees in Jesus the promised "wounded

---

[6] Jerome's Latin translation of the Bible (the Vulgate, fourth century) did this, as did the English translation of the Vulgate (Douay-Rheims, 1610) and the Wycliffe Bible (1382).

healer."[7] Thus Thomas Hanks can say: "Matthew does not focus on a secondary element in describing the Servant; instead he is dealing with a primary feature."[8]

WHY THIS HAS BEEN DONE

Why then do so many versions of the Bible miss or minimize this "primary feature" of Isaiah 53?

The tendency began as early as the second or third century BC, when the Hebrew Bible was translated into Greek. The Septuagint, as it is called, spiritualizes sickness, substituting the Greek word *hamartia*, sin, for the Hebrew word *holi*, sickness—"He bore our sin," rather than "He bore our sickness." But *holi* does not mean sin. The Hebrew of Isaiah clearly says the Servant deals with sickness; He enters into human sickness in order to heal.

Then why do some versions still miss or minimize this fact? Part of the reason is that nowhere in the four Gospels are we told that Jesus, the fulfillment of Isaiah 53, was ever sick. We are told that He agonized so much in the garden of Gethsemane that He sweat drops of blood. We are told that when someone who was sick touched Him, life seemed to drain out of Him (Mark 5:30). We know that both before being nailed to the cross, and while on the cross, His flesh was ripped, and He lost a lot of blood. But nowhere are we specifically

[7] This phrase was made famous by Henri J. M. Nouwen, *The Wounded Healer: Ministry in Contemporary Society* (New York: Doubleday, 1972).
[8] Hanks, *God So Loved the Third World*, 77.

told that Jesus became sick. He may have—the writers of the Gospels do not tell us everything that happened to Jesus. But because there is no explicit statement that Jesus suffered sickness, the tendency to "spiritualize" the sickness thread of Isaiah 53 continues.

There is another reason for missing or minimizing what Isaiah foresaw. Many have assumed that Isaiah 53 only refers to Jesus's death on the cross, and that Jesus's death on the cross has to do only with sin. But, Isaiah 53 does not refer only to Jesus's death. Indeed, it refers primarily to Jesus's pre-cross life.

If Isaiah could speak to us to today, he would tell us that we are saved not only by Jesus's death and resurrection, but also by His life. That is, we are saved by the Servant. And His servant work is taking place in His earthly life; Jesus is saving the world even as He is living in the world. We are saved by Jesus, by the whole Jesus, by His life as well as His death.

A Cord of Three Strands

And there is one more reason for the "spiritualizing" of the sickness thread. The church, especially the Protestant wing, has tended to read Isaiah 53 from only one theological angle. We see only the substitutionary atonement thread, focusing on only the theme of forensic justification. The perspective many of us come from is that the chief work of the Servant is to take on the penalty for sin.

Now, that thread *is* there—big time. And we need

to hear it again and again! Isaiah 53:10 proclaims that "He would render Himself as a guilt offering." The Servant comes to offer the sacrifice that atones for the sin of the world. And wonder of wonders—He Himself is the sacrifice! The great Shepherd of the sheep becomes the Lamb of God, and "as the lamb of God he took upon Himself the entire punishment for sin and paid the just penalty by the gift of his sinless life."[9]

When we pay attention to the words Isaiah uses relative to sin, this thread of the gospel gets even more wonderful! For Isaiah does not use the garden-variety word for sin which means "miss the mark." The words he uses go deeper.

Isaiah uses *pasha*, which means "rebellion." For Isaiah, the human problem is not just that we keep missing the mark; the problem is that we keep on rebelling against God's clear will. The Servant comes to take on that deep-seated rebellion!

> "He was pierced through for our transgressions [rebellion]" (Isa. 53:5).
> "For the transgression [rebellion] of My people, to whom the stroke was due . . . " (Isa. 53:8).
> He "was numbered with the transgressors [rebels] . . . and interceded for the transgressors [rebels]" (Isa. 53:12).

---

[9] Robert H. Mounce, *A Living Hope: A Commentary on 1 and 2 Peter* (Grand Rapids: Eerdmans, 1982), 38.

And Isaiah uses the word *aon*, which means iniquity, that deeply rooted perversion or twistedness that makes us chose to rebel.

> "He was crushed for our iniquities
>   [perverted-twistedness]" (Isa. 53:5).
> "The LORD has caused the iniquity
>   [perverted-twistedness] of us all to fall on
>   Him" (Isa. 53:6).
> "As He will bear their iniquity . . .
>   [perverted-twistedness]" (Isa. 53:11).

The One against whom we have rebelled becomes one of us, and suffers in our place for our rebellion and iniquity.

We understandably get so caught up in this one thread of Isaiah 53 that we miss the others that are there. And there *are* others, even in addition to the sickness thread.

For Isaiah says the Servant also comes to set people free from oppression. A number of times he uses the words "oppress" and "afflict." The words refer to the oppression of injustice; the oppression of political and economic injustice. The Servant comes to set people free from *that* dimension of our brokenness too. "He was oppressed and He was afflicted, yet He did not open His mouth" (Isa. 53:7). He set the captives free by allowing Himself to become a captive!

And through this apparently foolish and weak move, He wins the victory over the oppressors!

"He will see His offspring, He will prolong His
   days" (Isa. 53:10).
"I will allot Him a portion with the great . . .
   because He poured out Himself to death"
   (Isa. 53:12).
"Behold [Look! Watch this!], My Servant will
   prosper, He will be high and lifted up and
   greatly exalted" (Isa. 52:13).
"Kings will shut their mouths on account of
   Him" (Isa. 52:15).

So Isaiah, who is in my mind the greatest of the
Hebrew theologians, sees the work of the Servant of
Yahweh holistically. He highlights three threads:

Thread one: the Servant comes to deal with the
   root problems of rebellion and twistedness.
Thread two: the Servant comes to liberate
   people from oppression.
Thread three: the Servant comes to heal.

The Servant does the first by identifying with us
rebels, and taking upon Himself the judgment the
rebels deserve. He does the second by identifying with
the oppressed, and letting the oppressive forces take
Him captive, thereby disempowering them. And He
does the third by entering into our sickness, and taking
it and carrying it.

Matthew has not twisted Isaiah's prophecy. Matthew
has simply brought out one of the three threads in the
Servant Song. Matthew sees in Jesus's deeds of healing

the Servant Himself taking and carrying sickness. "He touched her hand, and the fever left her," because He Himself took it and carried it.

HE TAKES AND CARRIES

I do not yet understand how it all works. Is it that as Jesus touches us in our sickness He takes the sickness into Himself, so to speak, storing it up? And then on the cross Jesus becomes not only sin but also sickness? Is it that He can take and carry our sickness ahead of going to the cross because He knows that He will deal with sin, and can therefore, ahead of the cross, deal with sickness? Is it that Jesus is able to take our sickness into Himself, and carry it, without Himself becoming sick? That just as His holiness trumps our un-holiness, so His health trumps our unhealth?

Again, I do not know how it all works. But this I do know. When we come to Jesus with any form of sickness—physical, emotional, relational, spiritual—He does not turn us away, saying, "I only see patients on Wednesday . . . and only if you have extended insurance." And He does not throw us back on ourselves, saying, "Here, do these five steps for a healthier you . . . and check in with Me in a month."

Instead, Jesus stretches out his hand, He reaches out His arms, and welcomes us just as we are. And Jesus takes the sickness to Himself, and carries the sickness as if it were His own.

We are never alone as we then watch for what He will

do. He takes and carries it. He takes and carries you. He takes and carries your loved ones. He takes and carries me. He takes and carries the whole human race.

So I invite you to bring what you are carrying to Him, and thank Him for carrying it.

5

Even the Wind and the Waves

Matthew 8:23-27

23 When He got into the boat, His disciples followed Him. 24 And behold, there arose a great storm on the sea, so that the boat was being covered with the waves; but Jesus Himself was asleep. 25 And they came to Him and woke Him, saying, "Save us, Lord; we are perishing!" 26 He said to them, "Why are you afraid, you men of little faith?" Then He got up and rebuked the winds and the sea, and it became perfectly calm. 27 The men were amazed, and said, "What kind of a man is this, that even the winds and the sea obey Him?"

Many of my favorite texts of Scriptures are those in which Jesus and His disciples are out in a boat on the Sea of Galilee. I am drawn to these texts for at least three reasons.

First, I have "life of the water" in my blood. I was born in the state of Minnesota, the "land of 10,000 lakes." I did not grow up there, but my family returned to Minnesota every summer to vacation, and the best part of the vacation was the time spent at the lake.

The second reason I am drawn to stories like this one is that I often feel overwhelmed—in over my head, about to go under. I can often echo the cry of the disciples, "Lord, we are drowning!"

The third reason for the pull of the sea stories is the most important. These stories, more than any other Gospel stories, pose the two fundamental questions of the Christian life. I used to think that we only needed to answer these questions at the beginning of the Christian life, but I have come to realize that they stand before us every step of the journey.

One of the questions is raised by the disciples, the other is posed by Jesus. The first question is one which, in one form or another, the church of Jesus must keep asking, especially in times of uncertainty and instability: Who is this in the boat with us? Who is this Jesus?

The second question is one which, in one form or another, Jesus keeps asking the church, especially in times of uncertainty and instability: Why are you afraid? Where is your faith? Where are you putting your weight?

The vitality of Christian living (and particularly the courage to joyfully obey) is directly related to how we answer these two fundamental questions.

THE STORM

Jesus had spent a long, long day teaching the

multitudes. He was weary, and He told His disciples to get into a boat with Him and sail to the other side of the Sea of Galilee. About halfway across the lake a fierce gale stirred up an unusually violent storm.

The Sea of Galilee is known for such violent storms. It is roughly 13 miles long and 6 miles wide, lying in a deep hollow. The surface of the water is 700 feet below sea level, and the lake is surrounded by steep ranges of hills rising some 2,000 feet above the water. The considerable difference in temperature between the top of the hills and the surface of the water generates turbulent winds that come swooping down the ravines, gathering enormous energy, so that they almost tumble in avalanches upon the water.[1] These winds can so churn the waters that columns of spray can rise above the mast of fishing boats.

Jesus's disciples were experienced sailors, and had often been caught in storms. But apparently this storm was worse than usual. Luke uses a word that literally means "hurricane." Matthew uses the word *seismos*, or earthquake. And the tough, rugged, macho fishermen were scared. The waves were breaking over the sides of their boat, filling it with water. They were sure they were going to drown. Have you ever felt that way?

They did everything they knew how to do. They hauled in the sails, they tied down the boom, they got out the oars, they rowed with all their strength. But

[1] The vivid metaphor is from G. Campbell Morgan, *Gospel According to Mark* (New York: Revell, 1928), 100.

71

everything they did was in vain. They were simply no match for the storm. All their training and technology simply did not help. A parable of the human predicament, is it not?

And what was Jesus doing during all the fury and turmoil? He was fast asleep in the stern of the ship (Mark 4:38). All three Gospel writers who tell this story (Matthew, Mark, and Luke) emphasize that Jesus was sleeping in the storm. It shows the real humanity of Jesus, underlining just how exhausted Jesus could become.

But it might also mean that Jesus knew something His disciples did not know (or had forgotten). In the Old Testament, "the ability to sleep peacefully and untroubled is a sign of perfect trust in the sustaining and protective power of God."[2] Does Jesus being asleep in the storm say something about His perspective on the ultimate power of storms?

Whatever it all means, the disciples woke Him, crying out three staccato words: "Lord! Save! Dying!" (8:25).[3] Their words reflect just how bad things were in their minds. It was not just, "We are in trouble." They weren't yelling, "We are about to topple," but, "We're going to die!" Jesus woke. G. Campbell Morgan notes:

> The rush of the storm, and the sweep of the wind did not wake Him; but the touch of the trembling

---

[2] D. E. Nineham, *The Gospel of St. Mark* (Baltimore: Penguin, 1963), 146.
[3] F. Dale Bruner, *The Christbook: A Historical/Theological Commentary, Matthew 1-12* (Waco: Word Books, 1987), 318.

hand, and the cry of men in trouble, did. . . . We have seen something of this glory in a mother, whom all the noise of traffic will not move, but who will be aroused by the sigh of a baby.[4]

DO YOU NOT CARE?

As Jesus woke, He heard from the lips of the disciples a plea that echoes through the ages. It is Mark who remembers the disciples crying out, "Teacher, do You not care that we are perishing?" (Mark 4:38).

The disciples' plea is more than just a call for help. It is a protest against Jesus's apparent indifference to His own predicament. Notice the pronoun "we." "Do You not care that *we* are perishing?" Yes, the disciples are part of the "we," but so is Jesus.

Matthew stresses at the beginning of the story that the disciples and Jesus are in the boat (8:23). The disciples feared their own death, but I think what concerned them more was that Jesus might die. And Jesus did not seem to care. He was not entering into their panic and fear. Let me paraphrase the disciples' plea:

Master, Teacher, You too are about to go under. Does that not bother You? Everything You stand for is about to go down the drain. Do you not care? What will happen to Your dream of establishing the kingdom of God? What will happen to Your plan to redeem the world and recreate

[4] Morgan, *Gospel According to Mark*, 102.

human life? Do You not feel the urgency of this situation? If we perish (and you are part of the we!) the kingdom is finished! Are You not worried, Jesus?

Have you ever felt that way? Have you ever thought that if the Lord does not do such-and-such right now it will come apart?

Jesus responds to the disciples' cry for help. But they were not at all ready for His answer. Jesus stood up— no small feat in a rocking boat. And then, without any fanfare, He spoke to the wind and the sea!

Luke says that Jesus rebuked the wind (8:24). The word is the same word used of Jesus rebuking illness and unclean spirits. Jesus simply uttered two little words: "Hush! Be-stilled!" Literally, "Calm down, be muzzled!" And within seconds, the winds died down, and the sea was perfectly calm.

WHO IS THIS?

What was the disciples' response to Jesus? Matthew says that they "were amazed" (8:27). Understandably so! Any group of human beings would have been impressed by this act. For all our technological advances, we still stand in awe of the wind and the waves. Though we can use the wind and the waves, we cannot control them. So we too cannot but be amazed by the Carpenter in a fishing boat simply speaking beyond-our-control forces of nature into submission. No magic words. No weird incantations. No appeal to a higher power. Just a word. Amazing!

But the disciples were more than amazed. Luke tells us that "they were fearful" (8:25). And Mark agrees: "They became very much afraid" (4:41). The man they thought they understood had broken out of their understanding of Him. He had exceeded their limited expectation of Him. So they had to ask that first, fundamental question: "What kind of a man is this, that even the winds and the sea obey Him?" (Matt. 8:27).

Mark that word "even": *even* the wind and the sea. These fishermen were Jews, steeped in the worldview of the Old Testament. They believed that only the Living One, Yahweh, the God of Israel, had power over the mighty winds and waves:

The voice of the LORD is upon the waters,
The God of glory thunders,
The LORD is over many waters (Ps. 29:3).

By awesome deeds You answer us in righteousness,
    O God of our salvation,
You who are the trust of all the ends of the earth
    and of the farthest sea;

Who establishes the mountains by His strength,
Being girded with might;
Who stills the roaring of the seas,
The roaring of their waves,
And the tumult of the peoples (Ps. 65:5-7).

Then they cried to the LORD in their trouble,
And He brought them out of their distresses.
He caused the storm to be still,
So that the waves of the sea were hushed.
Then they were glad because they were quiet,
So He guided them to their desired haven
(Ps. 107:28-30).

Given their perception of reality, is it any wonder the disciples were afraid? What kind of a man does what only Yahweh can do?

But there is more going on in their minds that accounts for the "much afraid." In that day, the myth was common that

> The original act of creation involved God in a desperate, but finally victorious, contest with the forces of chaos and evil, which were identified with, or at any rate located in, the waters of the sea.[5]

In the Canaanite version of the myth, for example, the world came into being as a result of a war between Baal, the fertility god, and Leviathan, the great sea monster, the god of chaos. To the first-century mind, the winds and waves represented more than mere meteorological phenomena. The raging sea represented that power at work in the universe that threatens human existence.

In the book of Daniel it is from the sea that the evil beasts emerge. So too, in the book of Revelation. The

---

[5] Nineham, *Gospel of St. Mark*, 146.

sea represents the power of chaos, which tries to move the orderly cosmos back into the dark void. The sea represented the powers of evil that seek to engulf life and suck it into nothingness.

No wonder they were amazed and much afraid. Jesus had just muzzled the forces of chaos with a word!

Does this explain why the storm that day was so violent? Was this storm more than nature's raging? Was it, in fact, the attempt of the powers of chaos to destroy Jesus? Many scholars, commenting on the response of the sea to Jesus's word, like to quote Saint Jerome: "Creation recognizes its Creator"; nature obeys its Maker.[6] But may we not also say that before Jesus spoke, the forces of chaos recognized an opportunity to overcome the Creator who was now in the form of weakness?

Matthew (as well as Mark and Luke) follows this story with others that demonstrate Jesus's authority over the out-of-our-control.

A man held captive by demonic spirits encounters Jesus. The man was being destroyed—the same word the disciples used of their experience. Whenever the man went into a demonic rage, no one was strong enough to control him. Jesus simply speaks another word ("Go!") and the man was free.

Then a father approaches Jesus. His daughter was deathly ill. Jesus goes to the house, but when they

[6] Bruner, *Christbook*, 319.

arrive, people inform the father, "It is no use, the girl is dead." Jesus enters the house and simply speaks another word . . . and the girl gets up.

Who then, is this, that even the wind and waves, demons and death, obey Him? That is the fundamental question the church must keep asking itself, especially in times of uncertainty and instability.

How we answer the question will determine everything else we are and do. He is a personal Savior, a compassionate Healer, a wonderful Counselor, the Champion of the powerless, the Liberator, the One who baptizes in and with the Holy Spirit, the great Reconciler, and the Sanctifier. He is each of these, and all of them. But He is more. The waves and the winds recognize the cosmic Lord.

WHERE IS YOUR FAITH?

There is another question. Before the disciples asked theirs, Jesus asked His: "Why are you afraid?" (Matt. 8:26). "Where is your faith?" (Luke 8:25). Jesus seems to be reprimanding the disciples, and that has always puzzled me. After all, they woke Him, calling on Him to act.

Do you think that the boat could have gone down with Jesus on it?[7] Could the forces of chaos have overcome the sleeping Jesus? No.

This is why Jesus asked, "Where is your faith?" Is it

[7] I owe this question to G. Campbell Morgan, *Gospel According to Luke* (New York: Revell, 1931), 111.

in the power of the storm? In the powers of chaos? Or is it in Me? The words of an old hymn express it well:

No waters can swallow the ship where lies
The Master of the ocean, and earth, and skies.[8]

If the Word made flesh is on board, the boat cannot go down. Not only does Jesus have authority over forces beyond our control, but those forces cannot conquer Him even when He is sleeping! Even in the times when Jesus seems absent, or seems to be asleep, He is in control.

Is this not the point the apostle Paul makes in Colossians 1:15-17? Paul says of Jesus, "He is the image of the invisible God . . . all things have been created through Him and for Him. He is before all things, and in Him all things hold together." In Him, and in no one or nothing else. "Where is your faith?"

I want you to notice that Jesus did not say to those "little-faith" disciples in the midst of the storm, "Look, you guys simply have to row harder"; He did not throw them back on their own human resources. He did not say, "You should have worked out harder at the gym"; He did not exhort them to build up their inadequate human resources. Nor did he say, "Hey, don't sweat it. Storms come and go, it's no big deal"; He did not sugar-coat the crisis, pretending it was not threatening their lives.

---

[8] "Master, the Tempest is Raging" ("Peace, Be Still!"), words by Mary A. Baker, 1874.

What He did was pose the second question of our lives: "Why are you afraid?" "Where is your faith?" In your abilities? In the other people in the boat? In the boat itself? In the power of the storm? In Me?

What are the forces, the circumstances threatening to overwhelm and engulf us? Do we believe that Jesus Christ is adequate for these? As a rule, we do not. The way we react to storms says loud and clear that we do not believe He is adequate. In our heads we think He is. We affirm His Lordship in our creeds. We sing it in our hymns. But when the storm brews, we seem to forget what we affirm.

Our unbelief is reflected in all kinds of ways. We fret, we panic. Helmut Thielecke once said, "Every care is a vote of no-confidence in God."[9] I worry and fret only because in that particular moment I really do not believe that the One who loves me is able to handle life. I worry because I have, at that moment, greater confidence in that which threatens me than in Him who is with me.

Feverish activity is another indication of little faith. We expend all kinds of energy, hold all kinds of emergency meetings, because unless we act now it will all come apart.

It was only when the disciples had come to the end of their resources that they finally turned to Jesus. Sound familiar? Why do we wait until we are over our heads to shift our faith to Him? Perhaps this is why

[9] Helmut Thielicke, *How the World Began: Man in the First Chapters of the Bible*, trans. John W. Doberstein (Philadelphia: Fortress, 1961), 131.

God allows some of the storms to arise. God leads us out into deep waters where the only thing left to do is make the shift.

I invite you to now personalize this text. What is the out-of-control crisis of your life? Ask yourself the disciples' question: Who, then, is this in the boat with me? Can He handle the storm? Or have I now found the one storm that is beyond His control? Have I finally met the crisis that He whom the wind and sea obey cannot overcome?

Jesus does not promise to keep us out of storms. How can He? Often it is His presence that threatens the powers and triggers the churning of the seas. Often it is the in-breaking of His new order that stimulates the upsurging of the waves. Thomas Torrance writes:

> It is because the Kingdom of God has already invaded this world and is breaking up the kingdoms thereof that evil is provoked to such extreme bitterness and to its final desperation.[10]

But while Jesus does not promise to keep us out of the storms, when we realize who He is, we do not need such a promise. When we realize that He is Lord of all, we recognize that "we are far safer in the middle of a storm with God, than anywhere else without Him."[11]

[10] Thomas F. Torrance, *The Apocalypse Today* (Greenwood, SC: Attic Press, 1960), 38.
[11] Jeremy Taylor in Morgan, *Gospel According to Mark*, 109.

6

One Little Word Shall Fell Him

Matthew 8:28-34

28When He came to the other side into the country of the Gadarenes, two men who were demon-possessed met Him as they were coming out of the tombs. They were so extremely violent that no one could pass by that way. 29And they cried out, saying, "What business do we have with each other, Son of God? Have You come here to torment us before the time?" 30Now there was a herd of many swine feeding at a distance from them. 31The demons began to entreat Him, saying, "If You are going to cast us out, send us into the herd of swine." 32And He said to them, "Go!" And they came out and went into the swine, and the whole herd rushed down the steep bank into the sea and perished in the waters. 33The herdsmen ran away, and went to the city and reported everything, including what had happened to the demoniacs. 34And behold, the whole city came out to meet Jesus; and when they saw Him, they implored Him to leave their region.

The story told in this passage of Scripture raises all sorts of issues! But do not let all the questions triggered by the story of the demons and the pigs divert you from its one basic truth. The main thing Matthew wants us to know from this story is the same as what he wants us to understand from the story of the calming of the storm (Matt. 8:23-27): Jesus Christ has authority over all the forces that threaten to undo us.

Jesus of Nazareth, the Son of Mary, the Son of God, the Son of Man, the Suffering Servant, the Lamb of God who takes away the sin of the world, is stronger than any power that seeks to destroy humanity. He is able to free us from any form of bondage, and He can do it simply by speaking.

RECONCILIATION AND REDEMPTION

Since the middle of the last century, a dominant theme in Christian theology, especially in the so-called mainline churches, has been "reconciliation," restoring relationships. "God was in Christ reconciling the world to Himself" (2 Cor. 5:19).

The denomination I served before coming to Vancouver framed a confession of faith celebrating and expanding on the great work of Jesus Christ. The preface of this confession (of 1967) stated:

God's reconciling work in Jesus Christ and the mission of reconciliation to which he has called his church are the heart of the gospel in any age.

Our generation stands in peculiar need of reconciliation in Christ.[1]

Ours too!

Reconciliation with God.
Reconciliation with others.
Reconciliation with the self.
Reconciliation with creation.

But since the early 1980s I have concluded that our
age is in peculiar need of the work of Jesus Christ that
precedes reconciliation. What our world needs even
more than reconciliation is redemption—liberation
from habits, attitudes, patterns of thinking, forces, and
powers that hold humanity hostage.

In His first formal sermon, Jesus declares: "The
Spirit of the Lord is upon Me. . . . He has sent Me to
proclaim release to the captives . . . to set free those who
are oppressed" (Luke 4:18-19). Before we can enjoy the
benefits of reconciliation, we need to experience the
reality of redemption.

This is precisely what Jesus's gospel is all about. The
good news for our age is that "the kingdom of God
has come near." In Jesus, the emancipating power of
the Living God is breaking into the hostage compound
and setting prisoners free.

---

[1] "The Confession of 1967," in *The Constitution of the Presbyterian
Church (USA), Part I: Book of Confessions* (Louisville, KY: Office of the
General Assembly Presbyterian Church [USA], 1996), 262 (9.06).

Again, do not let all the questions generated by the text divert you from its one basic truth: Jesus is stronger than any power or force that seeks to undo us. Jesus can set us free from any power or force that seeks to hold us in bondage. And He does it simply by speaking, a fact especially important to affirm in parts of our world where people resort to elaborate rituals to ward off hostile spirits.

BIBLICAL STORIES OF DEMONS

What are we to make of the experience of the two men from the country of the Gadarenes? What are we to make of the other stories in the Gospels and the book of Acts that describe similar experiences? It seems to me that there are basically three options.[2]

The first option is to say that such events really did not occur. The Gospel writers have cast their portrait of Jesus in terms the people of their day would appreciate. Since people of that day believed in and feared the demonic, and since the Gospel writers knew Jesus freed people from fear, Matthew and the others created these stories hoping to alleviate fear.

The second option is to say that these stories are primitive ways of describing broken reality. In our day, we now understand that the phenomena first-century people attributed to demons can be explained in psychological or chemical terms.

---

[2] I develop this more fully in ch. 6 of my book *Who is Jesus?* (Vancouver, BC: Regent College Publishing, 2011).

Jesus, wishing to meet people where they are, accommodated Himself to their understanding of the world. Since people believed that some of their pains and disorder were caused by demonic agents, Jesus met them at their level of understanding. Instead of trying to change their basic worldview, Jesus entered it, even though He Himself did not hold such a primitive understanding of life.

The third option is to take such New Testament stories at face value, to say that the New Testament writers are describing the way things "really are" in a broken world. It is to say that although they cannot be described with scientific precision, there are such things as unclean spirits and demons.

This third option says that these spiritual entities can gain a measure of influence over people and cultures and cause all kinds of trouble. Such beings are "particular manifestations of the evil in the world that is hostile to God (see particularly Revelation 16:13-14)."[3] Just as the Living God has spiritual beings called angels to do His bidding, so the enemy of God, the devil, has spiritual beings to do his bidding.

This third option asserts that Jesus never "accommodated Himself to anything He regarded as superstition or error."[4] Jesus never hesitated to correct what He regarded as a wrong view of reality. "You will know the truth," He said, "and the truth will make you free"

[3] James D. G. Dunn and Graham H. Twelftree, "Demon-Possession and Exorcism in the New Testament," *Churchman*, 94, no. 3 (1980): 216.
[4] Bob Whitaker, friend and mentor, from a personal conversation.

(John 8:32). This third option reminds us that one of the express purposes of the incarnation was to destroy the works of the evil one (1 John 3:8).

As I have said on other occasions, I have been "dragged kicking and screaming" to this third option. I would rather that the facts led to some form of the second option, which would be a whole lot less complex. If this were the case, I could avoid a host of tough questions. Questions like:

> How does this concept of the demonic relate to
>   the insights of modern psychological physics?
> Can these entities still get a hold on people?
> If they do, how can we discern when that is
>   the case?
> And, if it is the case, how are we to act?

Two facts about the New Testament stories help me accept them as accurate descriptions of objective reality. The first is that the New Testament does not attribute all evil, all unexplained illness, or all weird disorders to demonic agents or spirits. The writers of the Gospels recognize maladies such as fever, leprosy, paralysis, and they do not attribute these to Satan or to demons (Matt. 8:1-17; Mark 1:29-31, 40-44; 2:1-12; 4:19). The New Testament writers are simply saying that some illness and some disorders are due to the work of the evil one and his henchmen.

The second fact about the stories that helps me is that the stories are not told in the way stories about demons were usually told in the first century. "For example, there is no report of Jesus using physical aids" like burnt fish livers, roots, or incense.[5] Furthermore, Jesus does not use any magic words or incantations. Jesus does not even pray or invoke any other name or power. He simply speaks!

> "I command you, come out of him and do not enter him again" (Mark 9:25).
> "Come out of the man, you unclean spirit!" (Mark 5:8).
> Or, as He simply says in the text before us, "Go!" (Matt. 8:35).

THE BONDAGE

Matthew's story of the two men from Gadarene is the most dramatic of all such stories in Scripture, for he chooses the most extreme case in order to hold before us the authority and compassion of Jesus the Healer.

It is a terrifying picture of what evil can do. The men were so tormented that they had to be sent out of town to live among the tombs, in graveyards. The townsfolk attempted to protect themselves from the men's violent fits by binding them with chains. But the men would break the chains (Mark 5:3-4; Luke 8:27, 29). Superhuman energy was at work in them.

Mark tells the story mentioning only one of the men, and describes how the man could be seen running around

[5] Dunn and Twelftree, "Demon-Possession," 214.

the tombs "wildly shrieking, cutting his flesh with sharp stones, attempting to destroy himself and bring to an end the torment of an unbearable existence."[6] The behavior was so wild and so terrifying that Matthew says, "No one could pass by that way" (Matt. 8:28).

What we learn from this event, and others like it, is that the powers of evil seek to distort the image of God in humanity. William Foerster, a German New Testament scholar, makes this observation:

> In most of the stories of possession what is at issue is not merely sickness, but a destruction and distortion of the divine likeness of man according to creation. The center of personality, the volitional and active ego, is impaired by alien powers which seek to ruin the man and sometimes drive him to self-destruction (Mark 5:5). The ego is so impaired that the spirits speak through him.[7]

That is what the powers do. They want to utterly destroy. This is the point of Jesus allowing the demons to enter the pigs. Do not worry about the pigs! On anyone's scale of values the men are worth more than the pigs.[8] Jesus allows the demons to enter the pigs "to indicate beyond question that their real purpose was

---

[6] William Lane, *The Gospel According to Mark*, New International Commentary on the New Testament (Grand Rapids: Eerdmans, 1974), 182.
[7] Given in ibid., 180.
[8] Ralph P. Martin, *Where the Action Is: A Bible Commentary for Laymen (Mark)* (Ventura, CA: Regal Books, 1977), 36.

the total destruction of their host."[9] Had Jesus not interfered, the demons would have done to the men what they finally did to the pigs.

How does this happen? How does a human being (or culture) get into this position of "being demonized"? Scripture does not say.

> We are told that playing around with certain kinds of magic and occult practices, or playing around with hallucinogenic drugs, puts one into contact with powers of darkness and deception.

> We are told that entering into certain religious celebrations focused on other than the Triune God brings one into contact with contrary spirits.

> We know that habitual sinful behaviors can become a foothold for the demonic.

But otherwise, Scripture is relatively silent.

THE BONDAGE BREAKER

I think the reason for this relative silence is that Scripture wants to put the spotlight not on the bondage, but on the bondage breaker, on the Redeemer.

The fact is, the powers of evil do the same thing. They too put the spotlight on the Redeemer (but for a different reason). In every one of the Gospel stories involving this phenomenon the spirits immediately recognize who

[9] Lane, *Gospel According to Mark*, 186.

Jesus is, and they know He has come to invade their territory and liberate people from their grasp. "What business do we have with each other, Son of God? Have You come here to torment us before the time?" (8:29).

The spirits know the gospel! They know that God the Son has come into the world to destroy evil. They are, however, surprised that it is happening before the last day. They recognize "the mystery of the kingdom," that in the Nazarene the future reign of God is breaking into the present ahead of the end of time. The spirits know the gospel: Jesus is stronger than they are and He has come to set captives free!

It is Mark who draws out the vivid contrast of before Jesus speaks the redeeming word and after he speaks it.

> Before, we see the hopeless torment of the man
>   and the utter helplessness of the townsfolk:
>   "No one was strong enough to subdue him" (5:4)
> After, we see that the man is "sitting down,
>   clothed and in his right mind" (5:15). And
>   the townsfolk become frightened in a
>   different way.

The basic truth of this Scripture is that Jesus Christ has authority over the demonic forces at work in a broken, violent world. As the people on another occasion said, "He commands even the unclean spirits, and they obey Him" (Mark 1:27). Or, as the disciples said after Jesus calmed the storm, "What kind of a man is this, that even the winds and the sea obey Him?" (Matt. 8:27).

THE IMPLICATIONS

Now, here is one of the practical implications for us. The "Lord of Hosts" gives His authority over the demonic to His disciples. Matthew, along with Mark and Luke, emphasize this fact (Matt. 10:1, Mark 6:7, Luke 9:1). Thus, when the seventy disciples return from their mission in which they announced that "the kingdom of God has come near," they run up to Jesus and say with joy, "Lord, even the demons are subject to us in Your name" (Luke 10:17). Jesus has given the church the privilege of exercising the liberating authority of His name. In the authority of His name the powers are overcome!

So, in the book of Acts, we read of Peter and Paul being used to deliver people from all kinds of bondage. In the city of Philippi, for instance, when Paul was going to the place of prayer, a certain slave girl began following him. She had a "spirit of divination" and "was bringing her masters much profit by fortune-telling." She kept following Paul and Luke, crying out: "These men are bond-servants of the Most High God, who are proclaiming to you the way of salvation" (Acts 16:16-17). She kept this up for days!

Finally Paul had enough. He turned around and said to the spirit of divination (not to the girl), "I command you in the name of Jesus Christ to come out of her!" (Acts 16:18). And the spirit came out, the girl was free, and the gospel broke loose in the city.

Again, I want to emphasize that the redemption

took place by speaking. No yelling, no mumbo-jumbo, no special technique. Just a word: "In the name of Jesus Christ, come out!"

This is why Martin Luther joyfully sang:

> Though this world with devils filled
> Should threaten to undo us,
> We will not fear, for God hath willed
> His truth to triumph through us.
> The prince of darkness grim,
> We tremble not for him;
> His rage we can endure,
> For lo! his doom is sure;
> One little word shall fell him.[10]

One little word. The name Jesus.

The church need never be afraid. The church can fearlessly move into the strongholds of evil, and in the name of Jesus set captives free. Jesus is stronger than any other power and He has given His authority to His church.

Later in Matthew Jesus says, "If I cast out demons by the Spirit of God, then the kingdom of God has come upon you" (Matt. 12:28). The word "come upon" means to "overtake," "outstrip." The gospel declares that God's reign of freedom and wholeness is breaking into the world and overtaking the kingdom of darkness.

---

[10] "A Mighty Fortress Is Our God," written by Martin Luther, based on Psalm 46, and translated by Frederick Hedge.

A PERSONAL STORY

I said earlier that I was dragged into accepting this dimension of the New Testament witness. Up until the early 1980s I tended to take the de-mythologizing approach: looking for "more rational" ways to explain what is going on in Jesus's ministry. But since that time I have had too many experiences that seem to confirm the New Testament portrait of life in our world. Through these experiences I came to realize that I had bought into the arrogant presupposition of the twentieth and twenty-first centuries: that our contemporary worldview is superior to the worldviews of other times simply because it is newer.

I want to share with you one of the experiences that forced me to accept the gospel stories at face value. The event took place in Los Angeles, California, on Thursday, December 8, 1983. Five people were involved, two couples and I. Both couples game me permission to share our experiences. They do not mind being identified, but I prefer to call them Mr. & Mrs. A, and Mr. & Mrs. B. The main person in the story is Mrs. B.

It was the night before a retreat that Sharon and I were to lead. We were not yet ready for the retreat, so we wanted to reschedule a meeting we had set up with the As and Bs. I called Mrs. A, at whose home we were to meet, to say that Sharon and I could not make it. She told me Mrs. B had just phoned to say she really needed to meet. So I agreed to come, but wanted Sharon to be free to stay home and prepare for the retreat. I told Mrs. A that I needed to leave as early as possible so I could get out to the retreat center and get a good night's rest.

As I drove to the As home, I was filled with fresh joy. I began to sing and worship in the car like I had not for some time. The presence of God was almost palpable. I felt as if the Risen Jesus was there in my car! When I arrived at the As home, I felt even more joy, and a deep affection for the people with whom I was to meet.

Soon after I arrived, the Bs came to the house. I could see fear on both of their faces. We gathered in the living room. Someone suggested we pray and get down to work. I said, "No, we have to sing some songs first!" So I led the five of us in the hymns and choruses I had been singing in the car. Then we prayed.

Mr. and Mrs. B proceeded to tell us what was going on. It involved Mrs. B, one of the most loving, sincere, sensitive, caring women I know. It seems she had been struggling with a bad habit. She wanted to get rid of it, so one afternoon, while working in her kitchen, she tried to let go of it, once and for all. She lifted her hands and arms in prayer, asking God to free her. She said she felt a peaceful sensation begin in her head and slowly work down her upper body.

But when the sensation got to her midsection, the feelings changed drastically. Instead of peace, fear. Instead of feeling relaxed, a tightening up. She said she felt like she was going into labor. Her legs tightened and began to ache. She had experienced a similar tightening at other times when she sought to deepen her commitment.

While in the kitchen, a frightening picture flashed through her mind. She saw one of her children being hurt at school. She stopped praying and went to call the school. Her daughter was fine, but Mrs. B was still afraid, and her legs were in pain.

Mrs. B turned to me and said, "Darrell, I think that some sort of evil spirit is in me." I was not prepared for that! My first thought was that Mrs. B was going to extremes. And I judged from the expression on his face that her husband felt the same. He seemed angry and disgusted.

So there we were. Five relatively intelligent, level-headed, modern Christians. And one thought she was in need of deliverance from an evil spirit!

I can still see the expression on Mr. A's face. He is a brilliant thinker, with a PhD from UCLA. He was the head of a finance firm in the city of LA, with a budget greater than most nations. He looked at me with a mixture of disbelief and concern for Mrs. B's frame of mind. An "I-do-not-believe-the-woman-is-saying-what-I'm-hearing" kind of look was on his face.

For the next two hours we talked with Mrs. B, exploring her thinking and feeling. My goal during that time was simple: talk her out of her self-diagnosis! Although I was coming to believe that evil spirits existed, I was (and still am) very concerned that people were attributing to spirits what is really to be attributed to their own sin, to their disobedience, to physical factors, to psychological needs, and to systemic injustice in the world.

So, as carefully and sensitively as I knew how, I tried to get Mrs. B to change her mind. I argued that although the Gospels tell of demonic agents occasionally causing physical ailments and psychological disorders (e.g., Matt. 9:32-33), such ailments and disorders could ordinarily be explained in other ways. And I argued that it is best to assume those other explanations first, exhausting all other causes before considering the activity of the demonic.

I was wishing I had with me Richard Lovelace's *Dynamics of Spiritual Life*. A church historian, Lovelace takes the demonic seriously. I remembered how he had described some of the havoc the demonic can work. But then he wrote:

> It needs to be said immediately that other factors besides demonic agency join in causing almost every aberration mentioned [in the description] above and that often there may not be any direct Satanic activity involved. As Puritan pastoral theory recognized, spiritual pathology can arise from four different sources: physical factors (illness, fatigue, malnutrition or what might today be recognized as glandular or chemical imbalance); psychological factors ("temperament"); fallen human nature; and demonic attack.[11]

[11] Richard F. Lovelace, *Dynamics of Spiritual Life: An Evangelical Theology of Renewal* (Downers Grove: InterVarsity, 1979), 140.

I told Mrs. B that much of our struggle, hassles, and frustration are simply the result of the flesh, our inherited sinful nature that resists the Lordship of Jesus. I also mentioned that many who think they need deliverance really need inner healing of painful hurts from the past.

So we spent two hours talking through all the other possible causes of her experience. The discussion seemed to relieve Mrs. B. She was willing to go back to the drawing board and ask the Lord to reveal some other explanation.

I have to tell you that I felt very good about my pastoral counseling—I had talked her out of her weird self-diagnosis. Mr. B and Mr. A seemed pleased too . . . and very relieved!

Since Mrs. B was by then more peaceful than when she arrived, I judged it would be okay to bring the meeting to a close and head off to the retreat center. So we joined hands for prayer. I held Mrs. B's left hand, her husband held her right.

Just before praying, I felt I should say, "Mrs. B, just to set your mind at ease, why don't I pray a prayer of deliverance. Then you can go home sure that there is another explanation for what you experienced." Everyone agreed.

So I prayed:

Lord Jesus. We know You are here with us to-night and that You are Lord of lords. I pray now that you will protect me and protect these my brothers and sisters, and protect this house. I pray that if there is an unclean spirit in Mrs. B that you would make the fact known and free her!

No sooner had I spoken the words than Mrs. B's body strained upward. It took all my strength and her husband's to hold on to her. She began to whine and moan. Her body began to twist and writhe. And her face became distorted, filled with terror.

I looked over at Mr. and Mrs. A. Their eyes were opened wide. I motioned to them to pray.

You know how I felt in that moment? You will think me strange, but I felt alive and full of joy. I could tell my face radiated with joy. I knew then why I had had that experience in the car. I had been prepared for this. Again the presence of the Redeemer was palpable.

So I said the first thing that came to my mind: "I order you in the name of Jesus of Nazareth to come out of her." When I said those words her body became even more contorted, her face even more miserably wrenched. I said it again, calmly and firmly: "I order you in the name of Jesus to come out of her!"

I did what I read the apostles did in the book of Acts. They did not rant and rave, they did not wave magic wands. They did not pray. They spoke to the spirits: "I command you in the name of Jesus Christ to come out of her!" (Acts 16:18).

The agonizing intensified. So I said the next thing that

came to mind: "I order you in the name of Jesus Christ, Lord of the Universe, to tell me your name. Tell me your name." Again the writhing and wrenching intensified. "In the name of Jesus, tell me your name."

I cannot describe how surprised I was when I heard something say "Bright." So I said, "In the name of Jesus Christ, I order you, Bright, to come out of her, to leave her alone, to leave this house, and to go straight to the foot of the cross of Jesus." I had remembered Francis MacNutt praying something like that in his book *Healing*. Actually, what he prays is:

> In the name of Jesus Christ I command you the spirit of {x} to depart without harming {the person} or anyone in this house or anyone anywhere else, and without causing any noise or disturbance, and I send you straight to Jesus Christ that he might dispose of you as he will.[12]

Then I said to Mrs. B, "Say Jesus's name. Say 'Jesus.'" She could not. I kept telling her, "Name the name of Jesus." Finally she was able to whisper it. Then I told her to say, "Bright, be gone. In Jesus's name, be gone."

She struggled to speak. Finally she said it. And all of a sudden, that energy in her body seemed to leap out of her and blew by me. And there came from her mouth the vilest smell I had ever smelled.

The writhing and the wrenching of her body

[12] Francis MacNutt, *Healing* (Toronto: Bantam Books, 1974), 203-205.

stopped. Mrs. B sat back on the couch. She was calm. Her face glowed. And she was obviously free. We all embraced. And then the four of us laid hands on her asking the Lord Jesus to fill her whole being with His Holy Spirit.

I looked over at Mr. and Mrs. A, the host couple. She began to smile. He was ashen. Rightly so! We had just witnessed an encounter with personal evil. We had witnessed the terror evil can cause. And we had witnessed the kingdom of God in power. We had received one more sign that the kingdom of darkness is coming to an end. And our worldview had been stretched!

After a little while debriefing our experience, and after another prayer for protection of the A's home, I left. It was 10:30 pm. I had to drive about thirty kilometers to the retreat center, and all the way I had to sing. I had seen the Savior overcome one of the forces that seeks to undo us. I had seen Jesus do what the Gospels describe Him doing many times.

I arrived at the retreat center. I visited for a few minutes with a team member who had stayed up to let me in. I went to my room and had the best night's rest I had had in a long time. What was I to fear? I had just seen the Risen Redeemer in action!

One basic truth: Jesus Christ is stronger than anything that has a grip on our lives. And He came to set us free.

7

Authority to Forgive

Matthew 9:1-8

¹Getting into a boat, Jesus crossed over the sea and came to His own city.

²And they brought to Him a paralytic lying on a bed. Seeing their faith, Jesus said to the paralytic, "Take courage, son; your sins are forgiven." ³And some of the scribes said to themselves, "This fellow blasphemes." ⁴And Jesus knowing their thoughts said, "Why are you thinking evil in your hearts? ⁵Which is easier, to say, 'Your sins are forgiven,' or to say, 'Get up, and walk'? ⁶But so that you may know that the Son of Man has authority on earth to forgive sins"—then He said to the paralytic, "Get up, pick up your bed and go home." ⁷And he got up and went home. ⁸But when the crowds saw this, they were awestruck, and glorified God, who had given such authority to men.

What is God's good news for a broken world? The gospel is a name and a fact. The name: Jesus Christ. The fact: in Him history has reached a major crisis point, and in Him a whole new order of life is breaking in upon the world.

In the event described in Matthew 9:1-8, Jesus draws us into the heart of his gospel. In it, we are brought into the very center of life in the kingdom of God.

As you may know, Matthew is not the only Gospel writer who tells this story. As is his habit, Matthew has abbreviated the story, paring it down to the bare essentials. I appreciate his intent! But without the colorful "extras" provided by Mark (ch. 2) and Luke (ch. 5), we do not fully appreciate the essentials on which Matthew focuses. Let us therefore go back into this gospel event through the memory of all three evangelists who proclaim it.

THE EVENT

The event takes place in Capernaum, which Matthew says is Jesus's "own city" (9:1). Capernaum was His headquarters during the early period of His public ministry, the town where He was most welcomed.

Jesus is in the home of a relatively wealthy man— we know this because of the tile on the roof, to which Luke calls our attention. As we approach the house, we find it, as Mark notes, overflowing with people: dozens sandwiched inside, and more clamoring near the doors and windows. They have all come to hear Jesus teach.

With a little creative imagining you can see the owner of the house bursting with pride. He has made the big time! Look at the size of the crowd! And look who is here—the new rabbi, the VIPs from Jerusalem, the teachers of the law (the doctors of theology), and the Pharisees (the protectors of the reputation of Israel's God). Everyone is all ears . . . except the owner who is too busy reveling in the glory.

Can you feel the excitement in the air? There's a high-pitched expectancy, as people hang on every word Jesus speaks. The religious leaders are critically analyzing everything this new rabbi is saying, making sure His theology is orthodox.

But no one has as high expectations as do five men who are outside the house. One of the five is lying on a stretcher. Apparently, they have heard about the amazing deeds of wholeness Jesus had performed in the area, and they were coming to Jesus for help.

The circumstances at the house present a problem: because of the crowd they cannot get through to Jesus. But the four men, as William Barclay says, had "faith that laughed at barriers."[1] So, up on the roof they go with the stretcher and the paralyzed man!

Houses in those days were essentially square boxes. There was usually a stairway or ladder alongside the house making it easy to get up on the roof. The roof

[1] William Barclay, *The Gospel of Mark*, rev. ed. (Philadelphia: Westminster, 1975), 47.

itself was flat, slightly tilted to allow for the rain, and was made of wooden beams laid close together wall-to-wall. The space between the beams was filled with tightly packed twigs compacted together with mud. If one had money, tiles could be laid over this roofing.

The four men are so convinced that Jesus can help their friend, and they love their friend so much, that they will stop at nothing, so they start to dismantle the roof!

Imagine how the owner of the house would feel about this. He is standing off to the side, lost in euphoria, when out of the corner of his eye he notices pieces of dust floating from the ceiling. Then more and more pieces, bigger and bigger clumps. And then a hole appears in his expensive roof!

Jesus stops speaking. Nearly everyone is looking up at the hole anyway. As the hole gets larger, through it, you can see four eager, expectant, hopeful faces. Finally, a rectangular object, 3 feet by 6 feet, is lowered through the hole on ropes. Everyone hopes the men outside are strong enough to hold the object! The object is lowered right in front of Jesus. Everyone can now see that it is a stretcher, and that a paralyzed man is lying on it.

The Scribes and Pharisees glance at each other. The owner is pale. The crowd is quiet, amazed by the audacity of the four friends. The four men stare down at Jesus, hearts pounding with hope. The man on the stretcher is slightly embarrassed, but glad to have survived the ordeal of being lowered through the roof.

Jesus looks at the four friends. He looks at the Scribes and the Pharisees. And then he looks at the paralyzed man. Finally, He speaks: "Take courage, son; your sins are forgiven" (9:2).

The doctors of the law and the protectors of God's reputation are outraged. "Why does this man speak that way? He is blaspheming; who can forgive sins but God alone?" (Mark 2:7).

The crowd is baffled. They have never heard this kind of speech before. The four men on the roof are dumbfounded—what does this have to do with our friend? He needs to be healed, not forgiven.

Here we realize again that, as C. S. Lewis portrays Him, Jesus Christ is "not like a tame lion."[2] We cannot come to Him with our agenda and expect Him to follow it. He will seldom act the way we write the script, which means He will often disappoint our expectations. But as Earl Palmer helped me see years ago, Jesus Christ only disappoints our expectation to fulfill our real need.

THE DISCOVERIES

Let's probe this event a bit further. In it we make a number of important discoveries.

First, we discover the purpose of the church. In the four friends, we have a picture of what the church is all

---

[2] C.S. Lewis, *The Lion, the Witch, and the Wardrobe* (New York: Macmillan, 1950), 180.

about—getting people into the presence of Jesus. That is all that mattered to those men, bringing their friend to the only One who could make him whole.

The church is to be a community of friends centered in Jesus Christ, helping each other move toward Jesus. Are you in the church? Do you know people who know you and know how to help you get into the presence of Christ? There are times when, like the paralyzed man, I simply cannot make the moves I need to make toward Christ. At those times, I need sisters and brothers to pick me up and carry me. I need the church.

In this event, we make a second important discovery. We find out the nature of faith. The four friends did not let the obstacles in the way deter them. They acted boldly and shamelessly, not caring what others would think about their actions. They simply had to get to the Lord. As Dale Bruner puts it, "Faith lives under one great compulsion: the determination to get into the presence of Jesus."[3]

Faith tears through the beams and twigs of time, pressure, and doubts . . . and lets itself down before the Lord. How we need to recover this robust determination! Far too often we give up too soon, and miss out on God's surprises.

We make a third discovery in this event. Jesus Christ is impressed by faith. The kind of faith exercised by the

[3] F. Dale Bruner, *The Christbook: A Historical/Theological Commentary, Matthew 1-12* (Waco: Word Books, 1987), 328.

four friends gets our Lord's attention. I am sure that when those men dug through that expensive roof Jesus smiled. Nothing pleases Him like people who take Him seriously and will stop at nothing to get to Him.

THE ROOT ISSUE

In this story, we also see that Jesus Christ is very wise; He sees through to the real issues of our lives. He sees through the man's physical paralysis to his need of forgiveness.

It was assumed in first-century Palestine that sin and sickness were inextricably related. You sin, and there-fore you suffer. You are suffering, so you must have sinned. A sickness or tragedy was thought to always be a punishment or direct result of a specific sin.

This is the issue in the book of Job. Job lost all his animals, servants, and children. Eliphaz, one of Job's "comforters" says to him: "Remember now, whoever perished being innocent? Or where were the upright destroyed?" (Job 4:7).

Jesus's first disciples came at life from the same per-spective. One day they met a man who had been blind from birth. They ask Jesus, "Rabbi, who sinned, this man or his parents, that he would be born blind?" (John 9:2). Jesus's answer? Neither. Jesus decisively rejects that simplistic view of life. Not all sickness or calamity is a tit-for-tat punishment for sin. Each specific sin does not necessarily receive a specific punishment.

Yet Jesus does affirm that suffering is the natural consequence of the power of sin at work in a broken world. All suffering is finally due to humanity's rebellion against God and humanity's attempt to live apart from God.

In Genesis 3, our first parents were tempted to take life into their own hands and to declare their independence from God. God warned them against such a move, telling them that they and the world had been created in such a way that only in dependent relationship with God do they and the world remain whole. Should they aspire to be their own Lord, the fabric of the created order would unravel. The first humans did not listen. They believed the lie that they could make it on their own, and as God said it would, their world fell apart.

So, although there may not be a one-to-one correspondence between a specific sin and a specific sickness, it is true that suffering is rooted in humanity's rebellion against God.

So, when Jesus says to the paralyzed man, "Take courage, son; your sins are forgiven," in what sense was that particular man in need of forgiveness? A number of possibilities have been suggested.

Perhaps he had in fact done something that directly caused the paralysis. Modern medicine tells us that envy, greed, or bitterness takes its toll on us physically. Or perhaps the man was living with unresolved guilt.

The psalmist understood this possibility:

> When I kept silent about my sin, my body wasted away through my groaning all day long. . . . My vitality was drained away as with the fever heat of summer. (Ps. 32:3-4).

Or perhaps the man was so steeped in the first-century view of things that he would be unable to hear Jesus speak of healing until he was first forgiven. The rabbis used to say, "No sick person is cured from sickness, until all his sins are forgiven him."[4] The man's paralysis may have had no relation at all to a specific sin, but because of his mindset he would not be able to embrace Jesus's healing work until the sin issue was settled.

Or perhaps the presence of Jesus awakened in the man a sense of guilt. When Peter encountered Jesus he fell down and cried out, "Go away from me Lord, for I am a sinful man!" (Luke 5:8). Maybe Jesus realized this and knew the man could not receive healing until the fear had been taken away.

Or perhaps Jesus is simply teaching the man, and us, that every person's greatest need is forgiveness. Yes, the man wants to be able to walk again, but what he needs more than anything else is to walk with God.

We discover here that Jesus Christ cares for the paralyzed man far more than the four friends do. Indeed, he

---

[4] William Barclay, *The Gospel of Matthew: Volume 1 (Chapters 1-10)*, rev. ed. (Philadelphia: Westminster, 1975), 327.

cares far more for the man than the man himself does. Jesus wants to meet the man's greatest need. Even if the man walks again, he is not whole until the relationship with God is restored.

Our greatest need is not food or clothing or jobs or health. Our greatest need is a relationship with the One in whose image and likeness we were created. What good does it do, in the final analysis, to be healthy or have "the good life" if we remain separated from our Creator?

Jesus disappoints the expectation of the four friends and disturbs the theological system of the scribes because He loves the paralyzed man enough to go to the heart of life.

AUTHORITY TO FORGIVE

There is another important discovery we make in this event. Jesus Christ has the authority to forgive. Jesus's word to the paralyzed man scandalizes the religious leaders: "This fellow blasphemes!" They realize that Jesus has taken on the role of the Living God:

> I, even I, am the one who wipes out your transgressions for My own sake, and I will not remember your sins (Isa. 43:25).

Jesus looks at the man and matter-of-factly announces that from this moment on all is well between the man and God. Who does Jesus think He is?

Amazing! In Matthew 8 we already saw Jesus exercise authority over illness—simply by a word He cleanses a man with leprosy, rescues a servant from the edge of death, and relieves a woman's fever. We have already seen Jesus exercise authority over the out-of-control forces of nature—stilling the raging sea with a word. And we have seen Jesus exercise authority over the demonic forces bent on destroying humanity—simply by a word He frees two demon-possessed men. Now He exercises authority over a person's relationship with the Living God, declaring that the Living One holds nothing against this man. Simply by a word Jesus here restores the divine-human relationship.

On what basis is the man forgiven? Did he do anything to make it possible? Did his four friends do anything to make it possible? No. All they did was come.

Jesus does not ask the man, "Have you kept the Law?" Jesus does not even ask the man to try to keep the law. There is no interrogation. He does not say, "My child, if you will promise to improve, I think I can work out some sort of amnesty." The man does nothing and says nothing. He is forgiven simply by the authoritative word of grace.

We who have been Christians for a long time tend to lose touch with the wonder of this word, and our lives show it. Let me paraphrase Jesus's word in several different ways to see if it comes alive again for us:

"My child, the Holy One, the One whose purity
    can consume, holds nothing against you."
"My child, I tell you that the slate has been

wiped clean. In place of all your sins is the
word 'forgiven.'"
"My child, I know that your debts are many,
and that you can never pay up. I tell you that
from this moment they are all cancelled."
"My child, the Judge of the Universe has already
taken up your case, and he has stamped on
your file the decree: 'full pardon.'"

How can Jesus say these things? This is what the religious leaders want to know: Who does this guy think
He is?

And Jesus takes up their challenge. "Which is easier,
to say 'Your sins are forgiven,' or to say, 'Get up and
walk'?" The emphasis is on the word *say*. Of course, the
easier thing to say is "Your sins are forgiven"—there is
no way to determine if the words accomplished anything! But you can test the effect of the words "Get up
and walk." Either the man does or he does not; either
Jesus's word performs or it does not.

So Jesus says the more difficult thing to prove that
when he says the apparently easier thing it really happens. "Get up and walk." And the man gets up and
walks. The word of healing brought the healing into
being. And therefore, we can be sure that the word of
forgiveness brings the forgiveness into being.

This is how we ought to view the miracles of Jesus:
they are signs that He has the authority to perform
the greater miracles of forgiving. C. E. B. Cranfield
says that "Jesus's healing miracles are sacraments of

forgiveness."[5]

Now, we who know the rest of the story realize that although it was easier for Jesus to say, "Your sins are forgiven," it was not easier to do. The forgiving of sin cost Jesus everything—it cost Him His life.

"My child, your sins are forgiven." Oh, how we need to hear these words again and again. The symptoms of not hearing them are all about us, in us, plaguing and paralyzing us. None of us has it all together; we have all fallen short of the glory of God.

So, I invite you to imagine that you are in front of Jesus. What is it that is paralyzing you? What is it that keeps you from fullness of life?

Hear Jesus speak to you:

> My child, I know everything about you. I know
>   everything you have ever thought, felt, said,
>   and done. I know what you are thinking
>   and feeling right now. And I say to you, you
>   are forgiven. Rise, take up your stretcher, and
>   walk in newness of life.

[5] C. E. B. Cranfield, *The Gospel According to Saint Mark* (London: Cambridge University Press, 1959), 98.

8

Faith in the Valley of the Shadow of Death

Matthew 9:18-26

^{18}While He was saying these things to them, a synagogue official came and bowed down before Him, and said, "My daughter has just died; but come and lay Your hand on her, and she will live." ^{19}Jesus got up and began to follow him, and so did His disciples.

^{20}And a woman who had been suffering from a hemorrhage for twelve years, came up behind Him and touched the fringe of His cloak; ^{21}for she was saying to herself, "If I only touch His garment, I will get well." ^{22}But Jesus turning and seeing her said, "Daughter, take courage; your faith has made you well." At once the woman was made well.

^{23}When Jesus came into the official's house, and saw the flute-players and the crowd in noisy disorder, ^{24}He said, "Leave; for the girl has not died, but is asleep." And they began laughing at Him. ^{25}But

*when the crowd had been sent out, He entered and
took her by the hand, and the girl got up.*[26]*This
news spread throughout all that land.*

I think you will agree that the story told in Matthew
9:18-26 has to be one of the most moving stories
in all of Holy Scripture. Indeed, it has to be one of the
most moving stories in all of human literature.

In this story, we meet two very different human
beings. One was a respected leader in the community;
the other, an outcast. One would have been welcomed
nearly everywhere he went; the other was shunned
everywhere she went. But though very different, their
paths cross in "the valley of the shadow of death" (see
Matt. 4:16).

She had been walking in the valley for twelve years.
He for only a few hours, since his precious twelve-year-
old daughter died. Both of them meet the One who
by His compassion and authority turns the shadow of
death into the dawning of a new day.

The story of the synagogue official and the woman
with a bleeding problem generates mixed responses
and emotions in us. On the one hand, the story awak-
ens hope: hope that the words "incurable" and "dead"
are not the last words. On the other hand, the story
seems too good to be true. Because the shadow of death
moves so relentlessly across the valley, what happens in
this story is almost too much to believe.

Here is human brokenness in the extreme, in its most desperate forms. And here is Jesus, Immanuel, God-with-us, meeting the extremes. Hope is reborn! And yet we fear opening up to that hope, lest it not be fulfilled in our case.

I invite you to work through this story in two movements. Let us first take a careful look at the way Jesus relates to these two very different people. Then let us examine the way these two very different people relate to Jesus.

> Movement one: focus on Jesus in the
> valley of the shadow of death.
> Movement two: focus on human faith in the
> valley of the shadow of death.

JESUS IN THE VALLEY OF THE SHADOW OF DEATH
Jesus's Style

What does Matthew want us to know about Him who is with us in our brokenness? Two major facts, the same two he has been holding before us in the other stories in Matthew 8 and 9: Jesus's compassion and Jesus's authority.

But before working with these two major facts, let me call your attention to two other facts about the Savior that we see in this text. First, we learn here that Jesus is a "conservative radical." Jesus preaches a radical gospel: in Him the time is fulfilled; the kingdom of God has come near; in Him history has reached a major turning point, and a whole new order of life is breaking into the world.

In the text that precedes this one he speaks of putting new wine into old wineskins (Matt. 9:14-17). The life of Jesus's new world order is so different from the old one that none of the forms of the old order can contain it for long. Yet that does not mean that Jesus jettisons everything of the old order.

This fact is seen in Matthew's reference to what Jesus was wearing that day. The woman touches "the fringe of His cloak" (9:20), or as other versions have it, "the hem of His garment" (e.g., KJV). The term "fringe" or "hem" renders the word (in Greek *kraspedon*, in Hebrew *tzitzit*) that literally means "tassel," which refers to the four blue tassels worn by the faithful Jew on the corners of the outer robe.

These tassels were worn in obedience to specific directives in the law (Num. 15:37-41, Deut. 22:12). People wore them to identify themselves as Jews and to remind themselves that they belonged to God.[1]

In later times, when the Jews were universally persecuted, the tassels were worn on the undergarment, and today they are worn on the prayer-shawl which a devout Jew wears when he prays.[2]

[1] William Barclay, *The Gospel of Matthew: Volume 1 (Chapters 1-10)*, rev. ed. (Philadelphia: Westminster, 1975), 347.
[2] Ibid.

Did Jesus wear the tassels on His robe so as not to rock the boat where it did not need to be rocked? Or does the way Jesus dress also teach us something about the spirituality of the new order—that we need tangible tokens and reminders of the things of the Spirit? Jesus is a conservative radical, conserving the dimensions of the old order that can nurture the radical life of the new.

We also learn in this story something about Jesus's style: He resists the limelight. Jesus resists the temptation to sensationalize the gospel. We learn this in the way He worked once He got to the place where the little girl was lying. The house was jammed with family members, led in their grieving by flute-players and professional wailing women. What an opportunity for Jesus to impress the crowds! But no, Jesus orders the crowds to get out.

I like Dale Bruner's comment on this:

> If Jesus had been a showman, or had had a drop of fanatical blood in his veins, he would have challenged the disbelievers to come into the room rather than to get out of it, so he could prove to them what he could do ("I'll show you something you've never seen before"). But for the Jesus of the synoptic Gospels, healing is not a show, it is not even intended to be an advertisement or attraction.[3]

---

[3] F. Dale Bruner, *The Christbook: A Historical/Theological Commentary, Matthew 1-12* (Waco: Word Books, 1987), 346.

Now let us focus on the central features of Matthew's portrait of Jesus in the valley: compassion and authority.

Jesus's Compassion

First, consider Jesus's compassion for the woman. From the Jewish perspective, there could be nothing worse for a woman than constant hemorrhaging. Imagine twelve years of continual bleeding. But the really terrible thing was not the bleeding, but the humiliation and isolation to which the woman was driven by the bleeding.

In Leviticus 15:25-27 we read:

> Now if a woman has a discharge of her blood many days, not at the period of her menstrual impurity, or if she has a discharge beyond that period, all the days [mark that!] of her impure discharge she shall continue as though in her menstrual impurity; she is unclean.

"Unclean"—that was the horror of those twelve years. The old law continues:

> Any bed on which she lies all the days of her discharge shall be to her like her bed at menstruation; and every thing on which she sits shall be unclean, like her uncleanness at that time. Likewise, whoever touches them shall be unclean and shall wash his clothes and bathe in water and be unclean until evening.

"Unclean"—everyday, everywhere she went, supposedly contaminating everything she touched. Can you imagine the psychological and spiritual suffering this woman endured? Twelve years . . . "unclean," "unclean," unclean."

It meant that she was ostracized from her own home. If she had been married before developing the problem, she had to be separated from her husband. If she had given birth, she had to be separated from her children. And it meant she was segregated from the synagogue, cut off from the worship life of the community, excluded from the fellowship of the people of God.

Most of the people in that town knew of her condition . . . and kept clear of her. This is why she sneaks up behind Jesus. She fears that if she approached Him directly He too would turn away from her.

Can you imagine the terror she felt when, after she touched Him, He turned around and looked at her (Luke 8:47)? She likely feared Jesus saying something like: "Woman, what are you doing? You are infecting everyone you have bumped into in the crowd. And now you have contaminated me! I am now unclean and cannot continue my work today! Woman, what were you thinking?"

But how does Jesus respond to her? What are the first words out of His mouth? Not "unclean." Not even "woman." "Daughter, take courage." Did she even hear the next words he spoke? Nothing else could possibly compare with or improve on that one word,

"Daughter."

> Twelve years of humiliation and isolation.
>> Then Jesus calls her "Daughter."
> Twelve years separated from family.
>> Then Jesus calls her "Daughter."
> Twelve years cut off from her faith community.
>> Then Jesus calls her "Daughter."

Jesus does not treat her as unclean. Jesus enfolds her with the word of adoption—"Daughter." Jesus, the purest of the pure, welcomes her into the family of God!

Consider also Jesus's compassion for the synagogue official. We learn from Mark's Gospel that the official's name was Jairus (Mark 5:22). Jairus was a ruler of the synagogue, elected to that position by the other elders of the community. He was the one who appointed the readers and prayers for the worship services. He was the one who invited the preachers. He had administrative authority over synagogue life.

This meant, of course, that Jairus was aware of, and supportive of, the mounting hostility toward Jesus on the part of the religious establishment. Was he one of those who charged Jesus with blasphemy when Jesus spoke the word of forgiveness to the paralytic (Matt. 9:1-8)? By the time of this encounter, the establishment had already made plans to eliminate Jesus. As a synagogue ruler, Jairus was no doubt sympathetic to the plan.

Then his daughter dies. Oh, how our feelings change when we enter the valley of the shadow of death. Out of great need Jairus searches for "the blasphemer." He then bows down before the blasphemer(!), and says, "My daughter has just died; but come and lay Your hand on her, and she will live" (9:18).

How does Jesus respond? He could have said to Jairus, "Well, well, Mr. Big Shot. You would have nothing to do with Me before. In fact, you were part of the plot to kill Me. Do you really expect Me to listen to you now? You really expect Me to come?"

Or Jesus could have said, "What kind of faith is this? Yesterday you rejected Me. You doubted My claims. And now, since you have nowhere else to turn, you come? You expect me to respond to this death-bed kind of faith?"

Or Jesus could have said, "Look, Jairus. You've had it good all these years. When did you and your cronies every really care about anyone else? Do you really expect Me to respond to your self-centered request?"

But what is Jesus's response? No word, but an action that speaks louder than words. Matthew tells us that Jesus "got up and began to follow" the man (9:19). Jesus does not reprimand Jairus. He does not extract from Jairus a statement of repentance. Jesus stops His teaching session and hurries off to Jairus's home!

Compassion. It matters not how we come. It matters not what we are or have been. All that matters is that we come. Jesus responds to whoever comes, however inadequate the motive or understanding of Him. Compassion.

Jesus's Authority

Focus now on the other central feature of Matthew's portrait of Jesus: His authority. Consider first Jesus's authority on behalf of the woman. Matthew emphasizes the length of the woman's suffering: twelve years (9:20).

Luke, the medical doctor, adds that she "could not be healed by anyone" (8:43). Mark takes it even further, somewhat tactlessly adding that she "had endured much at the hands of many physicians, and had spent all that she had and was not helped at all, but rather had grown worse" (5:26). The point all three evangelists are stressing is that the woman had exhausted all known resources; she and the medical professionals had done everything imaginable. Her condition was "incurable."

The word stabs like a sharp, cold knife:

> "I am sorry, Ma'am, but there is nothing more we can do."

> "But there has to be something you can try!"

> "I am sorry, but we just do not have the technology at this point in time."

> "When will you have it?"

> "I do not know. I am sorry, really I am."

Then Jesus enters the picture. "'Daughter, take courage; your faith has made you well.' At once the woman was made well" (9:22). Nothing is incurable for the Great Physician. Twelve years of misery ended in an instant, relieved the moment her faith touched the Lord who comes to recreate the broken world.

Why then does He not always do it? Why does He sometimes not cure the incurable? It is a tough question, and I never want to minimize it. But what Matthew wants us to see is that Jesus Christ can do what medical technology cannot do and what it may never be able to do.

Consider also His authority on behalf of Jairus. Jesus goes to the house. By the time He gets there, the grieving was at high-pitch: people rending their garments, flute-players and wailing women in "noisy disorder" (9:23). Jesus orders them all out of the house saying, "The girl has not died, but is asleep" (9:24). The crowd laughs . . . just as it still does when Jesus still makes His audacious claims in the face of the great enemy.

What did He mean when he said, she "has not died, but is asleep"? He said the same thing when He and His disciples received word of the death of Lazarus: "Our friend Lazarus has fallen asleep" (John 11:11).

Some suggest that the girl had not died but was only in a coma-like state, which Jairus and the community wrongly diagnosed as death. William Barclay notes,

In the east, cataleptic coma was by no means uncommon. Burial in the east follows death very quickly, because the climate makes it necessary. . . . Because of the commonness of this state of coma and because of the commonness of speedy burial, not infrequently people were buried alive as the evidence of the tombs shows.[4]

So, some argue that in the story we have an example "not so much of divine healing as of divine diagnosis; and that Jesus saved this girl from a terrible end."[5]

Is this why Jesus responds so quickly to Jairus? Did He know that the little girl was going to be buried alive? If that were the case, it seems to me that Jesus would have wanted the crowds to stay in the house. It seems He would have wanted to help them to be more careful in their diagnoses so that persons were not buried alive.

Clearly Matthew believes that the girl was really dead. So do Mark and Luke who also describe this event (see especially Luke 8:53). John believed Lazarus was dead even though Jesus uses the word "sleep" in that case. So what does Jesus mean "she is asleep"? I think an older New Testament scholar answers the question best:

> If Jesus says the little girl "sleeps," it is not because he believes she is still living, nor that death is just a sleep for him; he means that God, by [Jesus's] ministry, is going to show that death is not that absolutely irreparable thing of which men [people] are so frightened.[6]

[4] Barclay, *Gospel of Matthew*, 345.
[5] Ibid.
[6] Bonnard, cited by Bruner, *Christbook*, 346.

Jesus is announcing the gospel, the good news that in Him, and because of Him, death has lost its finality. In restoring the life of the little girl, Jesus was giving a sign of that fact. This act pointed to the greater act, when on Easter morning the crucified Jesus emerges from the tomb. In Jairus's home that day, Jesus "gave notice of his far-reaching purposes and the full implications of them."[7]

As Jesus Christ has authority over out-of-control forces of nature like the wind and the sea, and as He has authority over the power of evil, so also has He authority over death. He "took her by the hand, and the girl got up" (9:25).

HUMAN FAITH IN THE VALLEY OF THE SHADOW OF DEATH
Dynamics of Human Faith

We are now ready for the second movement. Look at how the woman and Jairus relate to the One who has entered the valley of the shadow of death. Consider the dynamics of human faith at work in the story.

First, faith is born out of need. It seems that neither of these two people would have made their way toward Jesus had they not had a need for which there was no other help. The woman had spent all she had. The man, I would assume, had tried every other avenue open to

---

[7] Michael Harper, *The Healings of Jesus* (Downers Grove: InterVarsity, 1986), 71.

him. How many of us begin the journey with Jesus Christ simply because He is worthy to be followed? More often than not, what sets us on the path toward Him is our need.

Up until the day his daughter died, Jairus would have never dreamed of getting close to Jesus. Why should he? Everything was going well for him. He had it made. He had the respect of his colleagues and community. And besides, Jesus had challenged most of his presuppositions about life. Why get close to someone who will upset your worldview?

Then his world fell apart: Jairus's precious daughter dies. And because she "means more to him than interpretation of the Law or his standing in the synagogue," he moves in a direction he otherwise would not.[8] Sooner or later, we all come to the place where nothing else works.

This leads to another dynamic of faith played out in the story: faith is born of hearing about Jesus. Need only generates the search for help. Hearing the word about the Savior moves the search in His direction. The woman apparently heard the rumors of how this man did not treat women the way others did. Jairus, as a ruler of the synagogue, was very aware of Jesus's audacious claims and scandalous deeds. What they heard about Jesus matched their needs! And therefore, they move in His direction.

[8] David L. McKenna, *Mark*, The Communicator's Commentary (Waco: Word, 1982), 118.

This leads us to yet another dynamic of faith in the story: saving faith is focused on Jesus Himself. Note the pronouns in each of the speeches: the man says, "Come and lay *Your* hand on her" (9:18). The woman says, "If I only touch *His* garment" (9:21). Faith is only as good as that in which it is placed. The issue is not the amount, but the object.

You have no doubt seen or heard the saying, "Keep the faith!" Good advice. But the question is, "In what?" Keep the faith in what? Or better yet, in whom? A person's faith can be totally irrelevant. Is this not the great tragedy of our time? At this challenging moment in history the vast majority of the world's population is placing faith in powers, ideologies, and systems, which are no match for the challenges.

This leads us to another dynamic of faith at work in the story: faith entertains the possibility of exceptions. The woman says, "If I *only* touch his garment, I will get well." The man says, "My daughter has just died; *but* come and lay Your hand on her, and she will live."

Faith faces the hard, harsh, tangible realities of the situation, and then sets those realities up against a bigger reality. As I like to put it, faith is fully realistic. In fact, only faith is fully realistic, for faith takes into consideration all the facts. It considers the facts measured by the eye and ear and hand, and takes into account the great fact of Jesus Christ. Faith defies the odds and gambles it all on Him.

This is the only way I can cope in our world right

now. The brokenness is so massive. The length and width and height and depth of it all is so painfully overwhelming. Faith says, "Broken—but Jesus, come and lay Your hand on it, and the world will be alive and whole."

This brings us to yet another dynamic of faith at work in the valley: faith takes any risk necessary to get to Jesus. The woman risks further humiliation and isolation. But it does not matter. She has to get to the Healer. The man risks his position in the synagogue, and his reputation in the community, but none of that matters. He simply has to get to the Giver of Life.

Do you want to be made whole? Do you want life? Of course you do! Then get to Jesus. Risk it all . . . and get to Jesus. When you finally realize that you do not have what it takes to make life work, and when you hear and finally believe Jesus does, you will do anything to get to Him.

This leads us to one more dynamic of faith at work in the valley, the one that seemed to thrill Matthew: one way or another, Jesus always responds to faith.

Matthew tells us that Jairus goes to Jesus and says, "My daughter has just died; but come and lay Your hand on her, and she will live." Then Matthew writes, "and Jesus got up and began to follow" Jairus (9:19).

Matthew uses similar words to describe his response to Jesus's call to discipleship. Jesus walks into the tax collector's office, looks at Matthew and says, "Follow Me!" And Matthew says that he "got up and followed

Him" (9:9). Jairus cried out, "She died, but You . . . " and Jesus rose and followed!

When Jesus calls us, we get up and follow. What else can we do? When faith calls, Jesus gets up and follows! He may not follow the road we want Him to follow, but He follows faith.

A woman wagers that for Jesus "incurable"
    is not the last word.
A father wagers that for Jesus "she is dead"
    is not the last word.
And Jesus follows their faith, and they find in
    Him life.

Questions still remain, I know. What about those times when we go to Him and He does not immediately cure us or raise our loved ones? I do not want to ignore or minimize the questions. But for now, let us press through the questions to Jesus.

Come with all the brokenness. Come and take Jesus and His compassion and authority more seriously than the brokenness. Today, cry out to Him, "Lord, lay Your hand on us, and we shall live."

Even though I walk through the valley of the shadow of death, I will fear no evil. For You are with me. Your compassion and authority, they comfort me.

9

Just Keep Following Him Home

Matthew 9:27-34

²⁷As Jesus went on from there, two blind men followed Him, crying out, "Have mercy on us, Son of David!" ²⁸When He entered the house, the blind men came up to Him, and Jesus said to them, "Do you believe that I am able to do this?" They said to Him, "Yes, Lord." ²⁹Then He touched their eyes, saying, "It shall be done to you according to your faith." ³⁰And their eyes were opened. And Jesus sternly warned them: "See that no one knows about this!" ³¹But they went out and spread the news about Him throughout all that land.

³²As they were going out, a mute, demon-possessed man was brought to Him. ³³After the demon was cast out, the mute man spoke; and the crowds were amazed, and were saying, "Nothing like this has ever been seen in Israel." ³⁴But the Pharisees were saying, "He casts out the demons by the ruler of the demons."

I want to once again, call your attention to the three verbs that summarize Jesus Christ's earthly ministry: preaching, teaching, and healing. All three verbs involve what Matthew calls "the gospel of the kingdom" (9:35). Jesus came preaching, announcing that the kingdom of God has come near. Jesus came teaching, explaining the good news of the kingdom. And Jesus came healing, manifesting the kingdom.

OLD TESTAMENT ECHOES

Now, Matthew is announcing "the gospel of the kingdom" in all kinds of ways. New Testament scholar George Beasley-Murray has observed that the affirmations of this text "ring a multitude of bells for Old Testament readers," sounding the arrival of the kingdom of God.[1] Matthew has chosen his words and phrases carefully to help his readers, especially his Jewish readers, see that Jesus of Nazareth is the long-awaited Messiah and that, as promised, He is ushering in the reign of God on earth.

Listen to the bells Matthew is ringing. "The harvest is plentiful" (9:37). In the Old Testament "harvest" is a metaphor for the dawning of the new age. Many times the Old Testament prophets spoke of the last days in terms of reaping and gathering (see for example, Joel 3:11-14). In using the metaphor of "harvest" Jesus is clearly announcing, "The time is fulfilled." The seeds

---

[1] George Beasley-Murray, *Matthew* (London: Scripture Union, 1984) , 44.

planted by the prophets throughout the centuries have germinated, and it is time to reap and gather the fruit. The surprising note Jesus goes on to sound is that those whom He calls to Himself get to be part of the harvesting! We have the privilege of being sent into the fields to reap and gather!

Another bell Matthew rings is this: "Seeing the people, He [Jesus] felt compassion for them"—His guts were ripped up—"because they were distressed and dispirited like sheep without a shepherd" (9:36). Here is echoed the great concern of Moses, that the people of God might become like a flock without a shepherd to protect and guide:

> May the LORD, the God of the spirits of all flesh, appoint a man over the congregation, who will go out and come in before them, and who will lead them out and bring them in, so that the congregation of the LORD will not be like sheep which have no shepherd (Num. 27:16-17).

This was also the concern of the prophet Ezekiel. Through Ezekiel, God laments that the under-shepherds He sent are not doing their job. So, in Ezekiel 34:11-16, God says that one day He Himself will be the Shepherd:

> Behold, I Myself will search for My sheep and seek them out. . . . I will feed My flock and I will lead them to rest. . . . I will seek the lost,

bring back the scattered, bind up the broken and strengthen the sick.

"Like sheep without a shepherd." Any Jew who knew their Bible would have heard loud and clear, "Here is the prayed-for and promised good shepherd. The Lord, who is your shepherd, has come to bind up the broken, to heal the sick."

Matthew rings another bell: "Son of David" (9:27). As Jesus made His way from the home of the synagogue official, where He had raised the official's little girl from the dead, two men who were blind followed after Jesus, crying out, "Have mercy on us, Son of David!"

"Son of David" was the most frequently used term for the Messiah in the first century. It echoed the promise God made to King David, that one day God would raise up a son of his, who would reign over an everlasting kingdom (2 Sam. 7:12-13; 1 Chr.17:11-12).

The men who were blind, because of all they had heard about the Nazarene, recognized in Jesus the fulfillment of God's promises. Here was the One who comes to reign. Here was the One whose reign is a reign of restoration and wholeness.

Another bell Matthew rings, the one he rings the loudest, has to do with eyes and ears, sight and speech. "Then He [Jesus] touched their eyes. . . and their eyes were opened" (9:29-30). "After the demon was cast out, the mute man spoke" (9:33).

No Jewish reader of Matthew's words would have

failed to hear what was being announced. According to the prophets, healing blindness and deafness was *the* sign of the King at work in His kingdom. Why *the* sign? Eyes and ears have to do with relationship—and the King comes to restore relationship.

Two men who were blind see! A man who was mute speaks and hears! (The word used here is *kophos*, referring to the double disability, "unable to hear and thus unable to speak"[2]). The bell being rung is from the prophet Isaiah, chapter 35, one of the most wonderful chapters of the Bible:

> Say to those with anxious heart,
> "Take courage, fear not.
> Behold, your God will come . . .
> He will save you.
> Then the eyes of the blind will be opened
> and the ears of the deaf will be unstopped.
> Then the lame will leap like a deer,
> and the tongue of the mute will shout for joy"
> (35:4-6).

"He touched their eyes . . . and their eyes were opened." "The mute man spoke" and heard. This means that God has come into the world to do what only God can do.

In all these ways Matthew is sounding the great note of the gospel of Jesus Christ: "The kingdom of God has

---

[2] F. Dale Bruner, *The Christbook: A Historical/Theological Commentary, Matthew 1-12* (Waco: Word Books, 1987), 352.

come near!" It is time for God's new world order to break into the world.

In light of all that Matthew is declaring, let us focus on the interaction between Jesus and the two men who were blind. So much about the gospel of the kingdom is revealed in the way these two human beings relate to Jesus. I call your attention to three themes.

EYES TO SEE?

First, the two men illustrate a dynamic at work in the whole gospel story: those who have eyes to see do not, but those who do not have eyes to see do.

The religious leaders, because of their studies and training, think they see. But they do not. What is their response to all the bells being sounded? What is their response to the deeds of Jesus? Do they, like the crowds, marvel and rejoice that people are being made whole? No! They grumble that the One performing the deeds is not acting the way the religious rules dictate. And tragically, they see in Jesus's deeds the work of the evil-one: "He casts out the demons by the ruler of demons" (9:34).

The leaders do not deny that power is at work in Jesus. How could they? What they deny is that the power comes from God. They are so locked into their own theological categories that they fail to see in Jesus the compassion and authority of the Living God. Those who should see do not.

But those who cannot see do! The two men who were blind were unable to see Jesus's form or face. Yet they see who Jesus is! In fact, these two men who were blind are the first people in the Gospels to see the kingly royalty of Jesus. "Son of David," they cry. They are the first people to use this title of Jesus. Yes, the title was fraught with ideas Jesus Himself did not embrace, but at least the two men recognize Jesus's true identity.

How did they see? We are not told. But somehow they did. Those who supposedly had eyes to see could not see beyond the surface. Those who did not have eyes to see saw beneath the surface, and realized the promised King had come! Again and again Jesus lamented: "While seeing they do not see, and while hearing they do not hear, nor do they understand" (e.g., Matt. 13:13). Two men without working eyes are the first to see who Jesus is! They see before Jesus heals them of blindness. Like so many I know who are blind, they see what I, who have eyes that work, do not see.

FAITH THAT GETS IN ON THE KINGDOM

Consider a second theme in the interaction between Jesus and the two men: the men illustrate the kind of faith that gets in on the in-breaking of the kingdom of God.

They cry out, risking further suffering by shouting out their plea. In that day, those who were blind were treated with disdain. And, sadly, they were banished to the sidelines. But these men recognize that something wonderful is taking place, and no one is going to keep them from getting in on it! Faith cries out, "Jesus, have mercy on me!" Faith overcomes the sophistication of the self-sufficient and sets aside convention to get to the King.

Then Jesus asked them, "Do you believe that I am able to do this?" Give sight? In faith, they make the great affirmation, "Yes, Lord." Yes Jesus, You are able, for You are Lord! How did they know this? Again, we are not told. But we can rejoice that somehow they did.

Throughout the years, the church faces many crises: the crisis of finances, the crisis of a lack of volunteers, or the crisis of cultural dynamics opposed to the gospel of the kingdom. But the crisis in all the crises is the crisis of conviction:

Is Jesus Lord?
Is He a match for the other crises?
Is He able?
Is He able to do what He promises?
Is He able to do what seems impossible?
Is He able to reconcile?
Is He able to redeem? To liberate?
Is He able to restore to wholeness?
Is He able?

Jesus's "able-ness" is inherent in the title "Lord." To address Jesus as "Lord" is to affirm that He has the final word—in everything, over everything. The two men recognize that Jesus is Son of David *before* receiving their sight. But more: they recognize that Jesus is Lord and is, therefore, able to do what no one else can do. They have the kind of faith that gets in on the gospel of the kingdom!

The greatest expression of their faith lies not in their words but in their action. The two men begin to follow Jesus as He walks through the city, making His way home. They cry out to Jesus, "Have mercy on us." And what does Jesus do? Did you see this in the story? They cry out to Him . . . and He keeps walking!

That is, Jesus does not immediately answer their prayer. In the other stories in Matthew 8 and 9, Jesus responds immediately, but not in the case of the two men. He does not immediately speak or touch. He keeps walking home.

And yet the two men keep following Jesus . . . all the way to the house where Jesus is headed.

> It is a great faith that cries out, "Have mercy on us!"
> It is a great faith that calls Jesus "Son of David."
> It is a great faith that affirms, "Yes, Lord."

But it is an even greater faith that keeps following Jesus when He does not seem to be answering prayer.

WHY THE DELAY?

This brings us to the third theme in the text before us. Why did Jesus not immediately respond to the men's cry? Why the delay?

On the first reading, one could get the impression that Jesus had the same attitude toward blindness that the public had in that day. Sadly, and wrongly, the blind were ignored, even "branded as dead."[3] But we know from the rest of Matthew 8 and 9 that Jesus does not share such an awful perspective.

Then why the delay? Why not immediately respond to the cry of the blind?

Was the delay "Messianic"? That is, did Jesus not respond at that point because He did not want to publicly own the title "Son of David" just yet? At that time, the title was politically loaded. If Jesus had immediately responded to "Son of David," people might have misunderstood Him, and thought of Him (or thought He thought of Himself) as a political Messiah.

Or was the delay due to modesty on Jesus's part? Did Jesus not respond at that point in the story because He did not want to be primarily known as "the wonder-worker"? Did Jesus prefer to do His work in a more private setting, inside the house, rather than on the street?

Or was the delay due to Jesus testing the men's faith? Was Jesus testing their sincerity? The consequences of being able to see were both thrilling and scary. Their whole life would be changed. Were they ready? Did they really want what they were asking for?

Or was the delay due to Jesus's desire to draw the men to Himself? If He healed them right on the spot, might they not, as many people who are healed do, take

---

[3] Michael Harper, *The Healings of Jesus* (Downers Grove, IL: InterVarsity, 1986), 85.

their healing, and go off to live their lives apart from Him? Was Jesus, therefore, drawing them into the house, where apart from the crowd, He could begin to establish a more meaningful, personal relationship with them?

Is that part of the reason He asked them, "Do you believe I am able to do this?" He knows what is in their hearts and minds; He does not need anyone to tell Him (John 2:24-25). Did He ask the question to deepen relationship, to get the men to own the relational implications of saying, "Yes, Lord"? Is that part of the reason for the delay in healing?

Yet, in none of the other stories in Matthew 8 and 9 does Jesus examine or quiz or test people's faith. Indeed, He even acts where faith is shallow or non-existent! So why the delay?

I think it is this: in delaying the healing, Jesus is teaching the men, and the church of which they became a part, "the mystery of the kingdom," the mystery that the kingdom is "already, not-yet."

The King has come. And therefore,
    so has the kingdom.
But the King is still to come. And, therefore,
    so is the kingdom.

This means that the wholeness Jesus brings is, until He comes again, "already, not-yet." Which is to say our prayers for wholeness are prayed in that tension. "Already, not-yet."

Jesus delays the healing of the men who were blind to reveal the "mystery." Already "the time is fulfilled." But it is only the dawning of the new day, there is more to come. Already the in-breaking is manifest in our midst. But it is still in-breaking. This is why I use the present participle—"in-breaking." Not-yet-fully-broken-in.

The two men knew enough of the in-breaking to cry out, "Have mercy on us!" They knew enough of the in-breaking to call Jesus "Son of David." They knew enough of the in-breaking to say, "Yes, Lord." Yes, You are able. And they knew enough of the in-breaking to keep following Jesus even when He did not immediately respond. And that is the greatness of their faith.

They had to wait only a short time; maybe only a few hours, at most a day. But we may have to wait longer. The day has been dawning now for two thousand years.

So, from this the story of the men who were blind, we learn this about faith:

Faith means letting Jesus be Messiah and Lord on His own terms, in His own way, on His own timetable.
Faith means crying out, "Messiah, have mercy on me!"

Faith means declaring, "Yes, Lord, You are able."
And faith means we just keep following Jesus the Healer. We simply get behind Him, and keep following Him all the way home.

Thank God we do it in the companionship of the Holy Spirit! We keep following Jesus home, filled again and again with the Holy Spirit, the personal embodiment of the kingdom of wholeness. He is the already as we wait for the not-yet.

10

Joining Jesus the Healer

Matthew 9:35-10:1

35 Jesus was going through all the cities and villages, teaching in their synagogues and proclaiming the gospel of the kingdom, and healing every kind of disease and every kind of sickness.

36 Seeing the people, He felt compassion for them, because they were distressed and dispirited like sheep without a shepherd. 37 Then He said to His disciples, "The harvest is plentiful, but the workers are few. 38 Therefore beseech the Lord of the harvest to send out workers into His harvest."

1 Jesus summoned His twelve disciples and gave them authority over unclean spirits, to cast them out, and to heal every kind of disease and every kind of sickness.

U p to this point, we have been watching Jesus the Healer at work. We have spent time in texts of the Gospels that describe the wide range of His earthly ministry of healing. We have watched Jesus enter into different forms of human brokenness and bring about significant wholeness.

That is, we have watched Jesus cause the kingdom of God to break into the world. We have watched Him cause the future to spill into the present, heaven to invade earth. We have seen Jesus act with compassion and authority in the very kinds of situations we all encounter in life on this planet.

In the text before us, we see Jesus the Healer pre-pare his disciples to participate with him in his healing work in the world. Up to this point, the discipleship of the first disciples had consisted in being with Jesus (Mark 3:14): getting to know Him, getting a feel for His vision of life, coming to terms with whether or not they could trust (and therefore, obey) Him. Now, the time had come to send them out in mission.

COMPASSION

Two facts about the mission Jesus sends them on stand out to me. The first is that this mission emerges out of Jesus's heart for the world. Matthew tells us that Jesus had been ministering in the cities and villages of Judea. And, looking out at the crowds of lonely, hurt-ing, desperate people, "He felt compassion" (9:36). We met this word (*splangkna*) in our first chapter—"the compassion which moves a man to the deepest depths of his being."[1] And we meet this word again and again in the Gospels (e.g., Matt. 14:14; 15:32; 20:34; Mark 1:41; and Luke 7:13).

Jesus saw the horrendous need of the world and was deeply moved—ripped up inside. He knew He could meet those needs, but could only be in one place at one time, so He said to His disciples, "The harvest is plentiful, but the workers are few. Therefore beseech the Lord of the harvest to send out workers into His harvest" (9:37-38).

The disciples felt Jesus's compassion and prayed for more workers. And, as is often the case, those who pray that God would raise up people who can minister . . . end up being the answer to their own prayer. Of course! For the closer you get to Jesus's heart, the closer you get to what is on Jesus's heart.

This is why we never have to fear that if people spend too much time with Jesus Christ in prayer and study they will not get involved in the world. The truth is just the opposite. The more time we spend in His presence, the more our heart cannot help but beat in time with His heart.

Genuine piety and radical social action go hand in hand. Piety that is only in love with pious experiences nurtures a retreat from mission, a retreat into pious

---

[1] William Barclay, *The Gospel of Matthew: Volume 1 (Chapters 1-10)*, rev. ed. (Philadelphia: Westminster, 1975), 354.

feelings. But genuine piety, piety that is in love with the Living God in Jesus Christ, always leads outward in compassion for the world for which Jesus died.

SUPERNATURAL MINISTRY

The second fact I want us to see about the mission Jesus entrusts to us is that it is a supernatural ministry. We see in Matthew 9:35 the summary of what Matthew has been developing in the rest of chapters 8-9:

> Jesus was going through all the cities and villages, teaching in their synagogues and proclaiming the gospel of the kingdom, and healing every kind of disease and every kind of sickness.

Then, in 10:7-8, Matthew relays to us what Jesus told him and the other first disciples to do:

> And as you go, preach, saying, "The kingdom of heaven is at hand." Heal the sick, raise the dead, cleanse the lepers, cast out demons. Freely you received, freely give.

Jesus calls His disciples to continue His ministry—to continue doing the very works He had been doing. He even said later that we would do greater works than those He had done (John 14:12).

As we have seen throughout this book, Jesus's ministry of preaching, teaching, and healing was a supernatural ministry. I should clarify what I mean by supernatural. It's not an ideal term, for to a believer in the Living God, what is natural includes God and His works. The believer's vision of reality is bigger than that of the secular, scientific humanism of our time. There is more to reality than can be seen in a telescope or a microscope. If one's vision of reality includes the Living God, then what most people refer to as supernatural is nothing more than an ordinary part of the natural.

But, though the term is not ideal, I cannot find a better one, and I am going to use it in the sense of "beyond what we can see with our eyes, hear with our ears, or measure with our instruments." But it does not mean "non-natural" or "anti-natural," for that would deny the reality of the incarnation. Supernatural means beyond human ability.

Here is the point relevant to doing Christian mission: Jesus Christ came into this world to do what no mere human being or collection of mere human beings could do. And Jesus Christ calls us, His followers, to continue doing that mission.

This is one of the keys to effective ministry: recognizing and remembering that we have been called to do something that requires resources beyond our natural abilities, and our professional training. When we talk about equipping and training each other to do ministry, we are talking about much more than grasping information and developing skills. We are talking about helping each other get in touch with, and become channels of, the Resource beyond ourselves. Unless we do so, all our information and skills will not accomplish the mission that Jesus Christ gives us.

The crucial verse of this passage is, therefore 10:1: "Jesus summoned His twelve disciples and gave them authority over unclean spirits, to cast them out, and to heal every kind of disease and every kind of sickness." Jesus Christ gives His disciples the very power we need to continue His ministry. Amazing!

This is one of the major themes that Luke develops in the book that we call Acts of the Apostles. The same power, wisdom, and love operating in Jesus of Nazareth has been given by Jesus to His church. Over and over in his Gospel, Luke says, "And Jesus . . . in the power of the Holy Spirit" did such and such (e.g., 4:14). And then, in Acts, Luke says, "And Peter [or Barnabas, or Stephen, or Philip, or Silas, or Paul] in the power of the Spirit" did such and such—and the such and such was what Jesus Himself did. The same power source that Jesus used to do His ministry while on earth has been given to His church to continue that ministry.

A good question we ought to periodically ask ourselves as a church is if Jesus were to remove His Spirit from us, which of our ministries would suffer? The ministry He calls us to do cannot go on with unaided human ability. We can only continue Jesus's supernatural mission in His supernatural wisdom, power, and love.

So, let us look more carefully at the specific aspects of our mission. Matthew summarizes Jesus's ministry as proclaiming the gospel, teaching, and healing. The ministry we are to continue is the three-fold ministry of preaching, teaching, and healing. Though these are distinct actions that can never be separated, it will help us understand our role better if we look at them individually.

PREACHING

Jesus preached, "The time is fulfilled, and the kingdom of God is at hand; repent and believe in the gospel" (Mark 1:15). The kingdom that the prophets promised would come at the end of time has come now. The blessings of God's new creation are now. This is what Jesus proclaimed with such joy: "In Me, the future is here. Not totally, but truly, here."

That same message is what we disciples have the privilege of proclaiming. "In Jesus Christ, the future has arrived, and we can begin to taste the new creation even in the midst of the old. Even now, we can know forgiveness of sin, release from guilt, and freedom from the power of sin." Wow!

Jesus gives this mission to each of us, not just to the professionals. Those of you who are not clergy have access to people and spheres of our culture that I cannot reach. You are the heralds of the kingdom in those spheres. You are given the privilege of blowing the trumpet to announce the King's presence.

You can see why this aspect of the ministry requires superhuman resources. Yes, we need help to get over our fears. But we need help for another reason. All the careful logic and brilliant rhetoric in the world does not, by itself, melt hearts hardened against God, lives so sold out to other kingdoms that they cannot turn around.

I am keenly aware as I preach that, unless the Holy Spirit is opening hearts and minds, my efforts will not get the job done. Jesus says to His disciples later in this passage,

Do not worry about how or what you are to say; for it will be given you in that hour what you are to say. For it not you who speak, but it is the Spirit of your Father who speaks in you (Matt. 10:19-20).

Unless the Spirit speaks in and through us, our mere human words will not get through walls of hostility, suspicion, and doubt.

This is no excuse for being lazy or sloppy in our work. On the contrary, we are to do our very best, to strive for excellence. But we must recognize and remember that even the best we have to offer does not accomplish the preaching of the kingdom. To do that, we need the supernatural resources of the supernatural Word.

TEACHING

Teaching is the ministry that follows up on preaching. Teaching involves expanding on the implications of the kingdom's arrival, spelling out the practical implications of living in the kingdom of God in this world. Jesus did this in many ways:

He taught the Sermon on the Mount (Matt. 5-7).
He taught parables, drawing pictures of the

character of the King and life in the kingdom
(e.g., Matt. 13).

He taught about how to get along in the
kingdom (Matt. 18).

He taught how to live waiting for the fullness of
the kingdom (Matt. 24-25).

Jesus has given us that same ministry of teaching. We are to teach each other (one-on-one or in groups) the ethical dimensions of living for Him in this cosmos. Again, this is not just the work of the professionals. We are all involved in this work.

Teaching takes many different forms, including modeling. The first step is to come to terms with Jesus's teaching ourselves. We need to study together and on our own. There is no shortcut to maturing as a disciple; study is essential.

Now, those of you who have taught the ethical implications of the Christian life know that this ministry requires superhuman resources. We do not change easily! We can teach the best we can, using all the tools of biblical scholarship, using the latest insights into interpersonal and group dynamics. But then we must remember to pray, asking the Spirit of God to open minds, melt hearts, and enable people to change.

HEALING

Jesus did not just proclaim the kingdom's presence and teach the practical implications of that fact. He went one step further, and set people free to live the new life of the kingdom. He healed. And He calls us to continue that work, with the scope of our healing ministry to be as wide as His (comparing 9:35 and 10:7-8).

This makes us nervous, doesn't it? We are to be agents of healing? Jesus wants to heal people through us? We get nervous because of the abuses of some healing ministries. We also can get nervous because we are not healed ourselves, or because we fear that if we were to ask God to heal, He would not.

Let me suggest a definition of healing that can help us get over this uneasiness. Jesus's healing ministry is always related to the kingdom; to heal means to remove the obstacles of new life in the kingdom. When Jesus saw an obstacle getting in the way of someone enjoying His new life, Jesus removed it.

Putting it this way may help explain why Jesus didn't (and doesn't) always heal in the way we think He should. It may be that Jesus judges the obstacle not to be in the way of the new life He gives. Isn't this what He told the apostle Paul in 2 Corinthians 12:7-10? Paul begged the Lord to deliver him from his infirmity, his "thorn in the flesh." The Lord said no. The infirmity kept Paul dependent upon the grace of God, so, in this case, not removing the obstacle actually enhanced new life in Christ.

Where the obstacle was in the way, Jesus removed it, and healed. If you study Jesus's healings, you find

JOINING JESUS THE HEALER

there are basically four obstacles he removed:[2]

1. The sickness of spirit. A major obstacle to new life is unconfessed, unrepentant sin.

2. The sickness of emotions. This is caused by the hurts of the past that damage our emotions. This obstacle is also caused by a distorted perspective of one's self, God, or both.

3. Physical sickness. This is the obstacle caused by disease, accidents, or not taking care of the body.

4. The work of the demonic. This is the obstacle caused by the enemy of God and humanity who can attack, hassle, and destroy people.[3]

The obstacles we encounter may have their root in any or all of these four forms of sickness. Praise God, Jesus Christ encountered each of them, and has healed them. In our study of Matthew 8-9, we have seen the full range of Jesus's healing ministry:

He sets people free from guilt.

[2] I owe these categories to Francis MacNutt, *Healing* (Toronto: Bantam Books, 1974), 146-147.
[3] If you want a first-rate, scholarly treatment of the demonic, I recommend Richard F. Lovelace, *Dynamics of Spiritual Life: An Evangelical Theology of Renewal* (Downers Grove, IL: InterVarsity, 1979), 133-144.

He repairs damaged emotions, fixing distorted
self-images.
He touches lepers and cleanses them, touches
blind eyes and makes them see, touches
paralyzed legs and makes them walk.
He drives out demons from tormented souls.

And, when you read the book of Acts, you see His disciples also remove these four obstacles in Jesus's name:

They exercised authority over the demonic forces.
Peter and John tell a lame man to "get up and
walk" and he does (Acts 3; so also Paul,
Acts 14:8-10).
At the city of Joppa, Peter raises the dead
woman Dorcas (Acts 9:36-43).
At Troas, Paul raises the dead man Eutychus
(Acts 20:7-12).

They were in touch with the same resources that Jesus
used to carry out His healing ministry.

Jesus has called us disciples to seek to remove the
obstacles that keep people from experiencing new life in
Him. And He gives us the wisdom and power we need.

One other thing I hope you have noticed about
Jesus's healing ministry is that He always discerns the
root of the problem. Physical sickness can have its
root in physical causes, but it also can have roots in
emotional or spiritual causes. To be effective healers,
disciples need to be able to discern the real cause—as
Jesus was. If we are to continue His ministry, we need

His discernment. We need His ability to spot the root cause as well as His power to remove the obstacle.

WOUNDED HEALERS

I want to make one more observation. Jesus calls us to be healers, but realizes that we are "wounded healers."[4] None of us is completely whole—physically, emotionally, or spiritually. We are "already but not yet," just as the kingdom is "already but not yet."

But we can be instruments of healing because we have been in the presence of the Healer. He has touched us, and that touch gives us something to offer others.

Jesus Christ sends out His disciples from His presence.

He sends us out as heralds of the kingdom from the banquet of the King.

He sends us out as teachers of the kingdom life from sitting at the Teacher's feet.

He sends us out to remove obstacles to new life from having had the obstacles in our lives removed by Him.

This is why I regularly stress the need for a personal time with Jesus. What finally motivates people to move out beyond their safe routines is their having been profoundly touched by Jesus Christ. If Christians aren't motivated to

[4] Henri J. M. Nouwen, *The Wounded Healer: Ministry in Contemporary Society* (New York: Doubleday, 1972).

do mission, they have not been with Jesus recently. And if we try to go out in service without the supernatural resources of Christ's wisdom, love, and power, it will lead to frustration, disappointment, failure, and finally despair.

As Henri Nouwen puts it:

> The basis of the mission of the twelve apostles was not their knowledge, training, or character, but their having lived with Jesus. . . . There has never been a Christian witness whose influence has not been directly related to a personal and intimate experience of the Lord.[5]

In the presence of Jesus we feel His compassion for a world in incredible need. In His presence we feel His touch that sets us free. From His presence we can go out to continue His ministry in His supernatural resources. And from His presence we go out in the spirit of His charge to the first followers: "Freely you received, freely give" (Matt. 10:8).

[5] Henri J. M. Nouwen, *The Selfless Way of Christ: Downward Mobility and the Spiritual Life* (Maryknoll, NY: Orbis, 2007), 14-15.

Afterword

In this book, we've been living in Matthew 8 and 9, and, at the start of our study, I said that Matthew presents ten mighty deeds of Jesus in these chapters.

This is true. But it is also important to note that Matthew the accountant has carefully and systematically arranged these stories. He has done so in three sets of three mighty deeds (by combining Jesus's interactions with the woman with the bleeding problem and Jairus's daughter).[1]

That is, Matthew has arranged them so that we see the following structure:

Three mighty deeds (Matt. 8:1-17)
>   Discipleship discussion: The cost of
>   following Jesus (Matt. 8:18-22)
Three mighty deeds (Matt. 8:23-9:8)
>   Discipleship discussion: The calling of
>   Matthew and new wine (Matt. 9:9-17)
Three mighty deeds (Matt. 9:18-10:36)
>   Discipleship discussion: Sending out
>   (Matt. 9:37-10:1)

---

[1] F. Dale Bruner, *The Christbook: A Historical/Theological Commentary, Matthew 1-12* (Waco: Word Books, 1987), 298.

The implication of this pattern is that you are not fully healed until you are a disciple. You can be cured of a disease, but you're not whole until you get up and follow Jesus.

And, the implication is that you can be not-cured of a disease, but be fully whole if you follow Jesus.

So, come to Jesus the Healer . . . and follow after Him for there is even more good news for Humpty Dumpty.

He Gives Us a New Past!

John 21:1-19

¹After these things Jesus manifested Himself again to the disciples at the Sea of Tiberias, and He manifested Himself in this way. ²Simon Peter, and Thomas called Didymus, and Nathanael of Cana in Galilee, and the sons of Zebedee, and two others of His disciples were together. ³Simon Peter said to them, "I am going fishing." They said to him, "We will also come with you." They went out and got into the boat; and that night they caught nothing.

⁴But when the day was now breaking, Jesus stood on the beach; yet the disciples did not know that it was Jesus. ⁵So Jesus said to them, "Children, you do not have any fish, do you?" They answered Him, "No." ⁶And He said to them, "Cast the net on the right-hand side of the boat and you will find a catch." So they cast, and then they were not able to haul it in because of the great number of fish.⁷Therefore that disciple whom Jesus loved said to Peter, "It is the Lord." So when Simon Peter heard that it was the Lord, he put his outer garment on (for he was stripped for work), and threw himself into the sea. ⁸But the other disciples came in the little boat, for they were not far from the land, but about one hundred yards away, dragging the net full of fish.

⁹So when they got out on the land, they saw a charcoal fire already laid and fish placed on it, and bread. ¹⁰Jesus said to them, "Bring some of the fish which you have now caught." ¹¹Simon Peter went up and drew the net to land, full of large fish, a hundred and fifty-three; and although there were so many, the net was not torn.

¹²Jesus said to them, "Come and have breakfast." None of the disciples ventured to question Him, "Who are You?" knowing that it was the Lord. ¹³Jesus came and took the bread and gave it to them, and the fish likewise. ¹⁴This is now the third time that Jesus was manifested to the disciples, after He was raised from the dead.

¹⁵So when they had finished breakfast, Jesus said to Simon Peter, "Simon, son of John, do you love Me more than these?" He said to Him, "Yes, Lord; You know that I love You." He said to him, "Tend My lambs." ¹⁶He said to him again a second time, "Simon, son of John, do you love Me?" He said to Him, "Yes, Lord; You know that I love You." He said to him, "Shepherd My sheep." ¹⁷He said to him the third time, "Simon, son of John, do you love Me?" Peter was grieved because He said to him the third time, "Do you love Me?" And he said to Him, "Lord, You know all things; You know that I love You." Jesus said to him, "Tend My sheep.

[18] Truly, truly, I say to you, when you were younger, you used to gird yourself and walk wherever you wished; but when you grow old, you will stretch out your hands and someone else will gird you, and bring you where you do not wish to go." [19] Now this He said, signifying by what kind of death he would glorify God. And when He had spoken this, He said to him, "Follow Me!"

No focus on Jesus the Healer would be complete without spending time in the moving story that the apostle John records in the twenty-first chapter of his Gospel.

As we noted in our opening chapter, human beings are complex creatures. There are many dimensions or layers to our humanity: physical, mental, relational, emotional, and spiritual. Because of the ruining effects of human sin, we experience brokenness in each of these dimensions.

And the good news of Jesus Christ is that He comes to bring healing to all the layers of our humanity. "Jesus saves" . . . means Jesus saves the whole human being. God created us to be physical-mental-emotional-spiritual whole persons. And He comes in Jesus to redeem and recreate us into physical-mental-emotional -spiritual-physical whole persons. This is what the kingdom of God is all about!

In the moving story before us we see Jesus bring about healing at one of the deepest layers of our being.

THREE-TENSE TRANSFORMATION

Clearly, the major news of the story is that Jesus is alive. The same Jesus who met and befriended tax collectors and prostitutes, fisherman and home-makers, Pharisees and Roman soldiers is alive! The Jesus whom we have watched heal leprosy, paralysis, fevers, hemorrhaging, blindness, and deafness is alive. The Jesus who freed people from demonic possession, and raised from the dead a little girl is alive! He is not "the late-great Jesus of Nazareth." He is the Living Jesus.

And because He is alive, Jesus transforms all three tenses of our existence. Because He is alive, He changes our future, our present, and our past.

We have a new future. Death is no longer the last word over us. It is only the second-to-the-last word, and the last word is Life, eternal Life. "Because I live, you will live also," the Living Jesus says (John 14:19). We can look into the future with hope. Nothing can overcome the Lord with nail-printed hands, which means that nothing can ultimately overcome those held in those nail-printed hands. Nothing of what threatens to undo us can undo Him. The Risen Jesus gives us a new future.

We have a new present. Every moment of every day can now be lived in companionship with the Friend of sinners, the Lover of our souls, the Healer. Contrary to appearances, we are never alone. Contrary to our emotions, we can walk into any challenge, tension, frustration, or crisis knowing that the Living Savior is there. Whatever we are facing, Jesus is at work, offering resources we ourselves do not have, making a way where there seems to be no way. The Risen Jesus gives us a new present.

And we can have a new past. As strange as that sounds and seems, the Risen Jesus can give us a new past. This is what we see Him doing for Peter the fisherman on the shore of the Sea of Galilee.

PETER

According to John, this was the third time Jesus manifested Himself to a group of disciples after His resurrection. The first time was back in Jerusalem, on the evening of the first Easter. The disciples (without Thomas) were huddled together in fear, behind closed doors. Without the doors being opened, Jesus suddenly appeared in the room, stood among them, showed His wounded hands and side, and said, "Peace be with you" (John 20:19, 21).

The second time was also back in Jerusalem, eight days after the first Easter. The disciples (this time with Thomas) were again huddled together in fear behind close doors. And again, without the doors being opened,

Jesus suddenly appeared in the room. He goes over to Thomas, who had said he could not believe unless he saw Jesus's wounded hands and side. Jesus offers Thomas the proof he thought he needed. And Thomas worships Jesus, saying, "My Lord and my God!" (John 20:28).

Then some days after that, this time in Galilee, Jesus again manifests Himself to Peter and six other disciples. And I submit to you that Jesus made Himself visible there and then for Peter's sake. The third appearance is all for Peter. Jesus shows up to bring deep healing to Peter.

Remember what the angelic messengers told the women at the tomb on Easter morning?

> Do not be amazed; you are looking for Jesus the Nazarene, who has been crucified. He has risen; He is not here. . . . But go, tell His disciples and Peter, "He is going ahead of you to Galilee; there you will see Him" (Mark 16:6-7)

"Go tell His disciples *and Peter*." Oh how Jesus loves Peter! And when He manifested Himself that third time, in Galilee, it was for Peter.

John tells us that Peter and the six other disciples had gone back to fishing. That is, they had returned to life as they knew it before Jesus had intersected their lives and called them into the adventure of discipleship.

Many students of John find it difficult to understand how people who had actually seen the resurrected Messiah would so quickly go back to their old way of life.

But is that really so difficult to believe? Look at us! We have not seen the Risen Jesus with our eyes. But:

> We know He is alive.
> We know that through His death He has
> conquered death and sin and evil.
> We know He is sovereign over all.
> We know that His kingdom is breaking into
> the world.
> We know He is the new Adam, the head of a
> new human race.

We know all that. And yet, we keep going back to what we knew before we met Jesus.

The fact that Peter and the six others went back to fishing makes the story all the more believable! It gives it what J. B. Phillips calls "the ring of truth."[1] Peter and the others were not prepared for Jesus to be alive after being crucified. He had told them, but they had no precedent from which to make sense of His claims. What happened did not fit their worldview; it did not fit any of their working paradigms. And, as is the case with most of us, their perception of reality did not change overnight. It took time to get used to the idea that the Man they watched suffer on a Roman cross was really alive. And they were not all that sure what to do about it.

So they did what most of us do when we are uncertain and insecure. They fell back on that which they

[1] J. B. Phillips, *Ring of Truth: A Translator's Testimony* (New York: Macmillan, 1967).

knew best. "I am going fishing," says Peter. "We will also come with you," say the other six (John 21:3).

In Peter's case, however, it was more than confusion that sent him back to the familiar. In his mind he was no longer worthy of relationship with Jesus. As far as he was concerned, he had disqualified himself from following Jesus into the new reality shaped by the in-breaking of the kingdom of God.

On that fateful night before Jesus was crucified, Peter had denied Him. Oh, all the other disciples had deserted Jesus, but Peter had specifically disowned his friend and master. And therefore Peter judged himself disqualified from discipleship. In that courtyard, just outside the room where Jesus was being interrogated, Peter disavowed any knowledge of Jesus. Not once. Not twice. But three times.

Luke tells us that Peter could see Jesus from the courtyard. And Luke tells us that after the third denial, Jesus turned and looked into Peter's eyes (22:61). Peter ran out of the courtyard, weeping bitterly.

Peter could not forget what He had done. He could not forget Jesus's eyes. He could not forgive himself. And the guilt, shame, and trauma over his past kept Peter from entering into the joy of the kingdom of God.

Peter believed that Jesus was alive. I want to stress that. The two appearances in the upper room made it clear that Jesus was really alive. But Peter was unable to enter and enjoy the new future and new present because of a haunting past.

So Peter did what we do. He retreated into that which he knew best, into that which made him feel comfortable: "I am going fishing."

Every one of us can relate to Peter's predicament. We all know his struggle, held back from the fullness of life because of unfinished business of the past.

> Some of us are weighed down by regret over past actions.
> Some of us are haunted by memories of horrible and frightening things that happened to us.
> Some of us are bitter about past hurts.
> Some of us are hampered by tapes whirling in our minds which keep us from experiencing the freedom Jesus brings, tapes about our identity; tapes that tell us we are only worthy if we perform at a high degree of excellence; tapes that tell us when we fail that we are losers, and are no longer qualified to walk with Jesus.

Peter was not able to freely enter into what he knew in his head to be true. He could not embrace the new future and the new present because of his unresolved past. And that is why the Risen Jesus manifested Himself in the manner described in John 21. Jesus appeared on that beach by the Sea of Galilee to set Peter free!

THE BEACH

I suppose Jesus could have acted to free Peter from his past while he and the others were still in Jerusalem.

169

But Jesus chose that day and that place. The beach by the Sea of Galilee was just the right place for Peter's healing. It was there that "Jesus had first made sense to Peter."[2] It was on that beach that Jesus first called Peter into discipleship.

About three years before, Jesus was teaching the multitudes on that beach. Luke tells us that after teaching, Jesus turned to the fishermen Peter, James, and John and said, "Put out into the deep water and let down your nets for a catch" (Luke 5:4). At first Peter argued with Jesus: "Master, we worked hard all night and caught nothing." He, after all, knew more about fishing than a carpenter-turned preacher, right? "But," said Peter, "I will do as You say and let down the nets" (5:5).

Do you remember what happened when Peter did what Jesus told him to do? The nets filled with fish—so many that the nets began to break. Peter was amazed by Jesus's insight and fell at Jesus's feet, saying, "Go away from me Lord, for I am a sinful man!" (Luke 5:8).

Can you recall Jesus's response to that sinful man? He called him to follow Him. Jesus granted the sinful fisherman the grand privilege of discipleship. At the beginning of the journey, on the beach, Peter discovered grace: Jesus Christ calls us to Himself while we are still sinful, simply on the basis of grace! "Do not fear," said Jesus; "from now on you will be catching men" (Luke 5:10).

[2] Earl F. Palmer, *The Intimate Gospel: Studies in John* (Waco: Word, 1978),177.

But that was three years ago. That was before Peter denied his Lord. And as far as Peter was concerned, that three-fold denial disqualified him from the business of catching people. Ever feel that way? I have many times.

Then, a week or so after His resurrection, Jesus again finds Peter on the beach. Do you see what Jesus is doing? He is taking Peter to the place where it all began. He is taking Peter back to the original encounter. He is taking Peter back to grace.

Now watch what Jesus the Healer does this time. It is brilliant!

Peter and the six disciples are in a boat about a hundred yards from shore. Again, they had been fishing all night. I'm told that fishing is best on the Sea of Galilee at night. But they had caught nothing. At daybreak Jesus appears on the beach. But the disciples do not immediately recognize Him (John 21:4). For one thing, they were not expecting Him to appear—not in the midst of their normal routine! Not in their workplace! For another thing, although it was the same Jesus they knew before Easter, there was something different about Him.

Jesus yells from the shore: "Children, you do not have any fish, do you?" "No," they yell back. Then He yells, "Cast the net on the right-hand side of the boat and you will find a catch." I can imagine the disciples saying to one another, "Where have we heard this before?" And when they did what the Stranger told them to do, the nets filled with fish . . . so much so they could not pull the nets into the boat.

Then it clicked for the beloved disciple. "It is the Lord," he tells Peter (v. 7). And true to his character, Peter immediately acts on the insight. He had stripped to his undergarments for work. Because it was the custom of that day to greet people in respectable clothing, Peter put on his outer garments and then dove into the water, swam for the shore, and headed for Jesus.

When Peter gets to the shore, he finds that Jesus had prepared breakfast for the group. Amazing, isn't it? Even after His resurrection, Jesus is still serving. Even in His glory He chooses to be Servant.

The Fire

Jesus had prepared some bread and some fish. And John tells us that Jesus had cooked the fish on a charcoal fire (v. 9). John is a very precise writer. I have lived in this Gospel since 1968, and I have come to trust John. When he makes reference to specific persons or places or objects, he does so for a purpose.

Why does John bother with this detail? Why does he deliberately call it a charcoal fire? Because the part of Peter's past which held him back from experiencing life with the Living Jesus was tied up with a charcoal fire.

It was while standing around a charcoal fire that Peter denied Jesus three times. "Now the slaves and the officers were standing there, having made a charcoal fire, for it was cold and they were warming themselves;

and Peter was also with them, standing and warming himself" (John 18:18).

Can you imagine the pain Peter felt when he reached the shore only to see a charcoal fire? Can you imagine the explosion of guilt and shame when he once again looked into Jesus's eyes across a charcoal fire?

It had been bad enough each time he saw a charcoal fire in Jerusalem. Each time triggered the replay of his past . . . "I denied Him." And each time he felt disqualified from Easter's new reality. There they stood, eye to eye, around a charcoal fire. Peter is "face to face with the friend he has denied and abandoned."[3] Can you feel the pain?

I believe Jesus intentionally built that charcoal fire. Jesus was forcing Peter to face the unfinished business of the past. Jesus was meeting Peter at the point of his past that kept him from moving forward.

This tells me that we need to be careful when we want to run from pain. Not all pain is destructive. Some pain is the doing of the Great Healer, and helps us toward liberation and wholeness.

Now watch Doctor Jesus work with Peter. Peter is staring at the charcoal fire. The tape starts playing again. Does he see that young slave girl serving refreshments to the officers who arrested Jesus? Does he hear her ask him, "You are not also one of this man's disciples, are you"

---

[3] Lesslie Newbigin, *The Light Has Come: An Exposition of the Fourth Gospel* (Grand Rapids: Eerdmans, 1982), 278.

(John 18:17)? Does he hear himself say, "I am not"?

While his past runs through his mind, Jesus catches Peter's eyes, and across a charcoal fire asks, "Simon, son of John, do you love Me more than these?" (21:15). What was Jesus asking Peter?

> Was Jesus asking, "Do you love Me more than these men love Me?"
> Could be, for Peter did try to out-love the others.
> Or was Jesus asking, "Do you love Me more than you love these men?"
> Could be, for these men were his best friends.
> Or was Jesus asking, "Do you love Me more than you love your boat and nets?"
> I take that option: "Simon, do you love Me more than that which you know best, more than that which makes you comfortable?"

Looking at Jesus across that charcoal fire, Peter answers, "Yes, Lord; You know that I love You" (21:15).

A tense moment. What will Jesus say? How will He respond to the one who denied Him? Will He rub it in? "You let Me down!" Will He say, "If you love me, then why, Peter . . . why did you deny Me?" Jesus, looking at Peter, says: "Tend My lambs."

What? Me?? You would trust Your lambs to me?

Peter looks at the charcoal fire a second time. This time does He see the soldier warming his hands by the fire? Does he hear the soldier ask, "You are not also one of His disciples, are you?" (18:25). Does he hear himself say, "I am not"?

Again, while his painful past runs through his mind, Jesus catches Peter's eyes, looks at him a second time, and asks, "Simon, son of John, do you love Me?" (21:16). And across that charcoal fire, Peter says a second time, "Yes, Lord; You know that I love you."

Another tense moment. What will Jesus say this time? Will He now say something like, "What am I supposed to do with someone like you?" No. "Shepherd My sheep."

What? Me? A shepherd for Your flock? That is quite a responsibility to give anyone, let alone someone who has failed You.

A third time Peter looks at the charcoal fire. This time he sees the slave who was a relative of the man whose ear Peter cut off. He hears the slave ask, "Did I not see You in the garden with Him?" (18:26). And Peter hears himself swear, "Man, I do not know what you are talking about" (Luke 22:60). "I do not know this man you are talking about!" (Mark 14:71).

And again, while the video of his past plays in his mind, Jesus catches Peter's eyes, looks at him, and asks a third time, "Simon, son of John, do you love Me?" (21:17). Peter was grieved when Jesus asked the question a third time because he had not yet understood what Jesus was doing . . . why it had to be asked three times. Looking at Jesus across that charcoal fire a third time, he says, "Lord, You know all things; You know that I love You."

Now what? Surely now Jesus will lower the boom. Now Jesus will rail on Peter, right? No. "Tend My sheep."

You are entrusting Your sheep, Your people, Your church, into my care? Oh, my.

And then Peter hears again, from Jesus's own lips, the words he heard three years before on that beach, the words he thought he was forever disqualified from hearing again. Jesus says, "Follow Me" (21:19).

Simon, I know who you are . . . I want you to follow Me. Note that Jesus has been addressing Peter as Simon throughout this passage: Simon, the real you, the not-yet-the-ideal you, I want you to be My disciple.

Do you see what Jesus has done? It is so wonderful! Jesus has healed Peter by giving him a new past. From then on, whenever Peter saw a charcoal fire, he would remember a different past. Oh, I am sure he still remembered that around a charcoal fire he denied his Lord three times. But from that moment on he would also remember that around a charcoal fire he had affirmed his love for Jesus three times.

From now on charcoal fires triggered a new video clip, one in which Peter sees Jesus cover the three-fold denial with grace! One where Peter sees Jesus restore the denier into relationship! One in which Peter hears Jesus commission him to shepherd the flock of God! Mercy!

The Good Shepherd found one of His lambs stuck

in the thicket of the past. And He healed him, setting him free to enter the new future and new present with a new past.

What is your charcoal fire? Where are you stuck? What holds you back from entering more fully into the life of the Living Jesus? Just for now, stand around that charcoal fire. Ask Jesus the Healer to heal you. In that guilt, in that shame, in that bitterness; in that hurt, abuse, trauma, failure; in that wrong decision, in that painful memory, in that whirling video, say, "Living Jesus, meet me where I am stuck . . . and set me free."

Questions for Small Group Studies

Several of my colleagues while serving at First Baptist Church (Abraham Han, Susie Senner, and Doug Liao) helped me with these questions for small group discussion.

Chapter 1: Jesus the Healer
1. Read Matthew 4:12-17; 4:23-25; 9:35-10:1. What leaps out at you? What questions do you have?
2. Why do these passages hold teaching, preaching, and healing so closely together in Jesus's ministry? What do these three aspects reveal to us about the kingdom of God?
3. How does Matthew describe the crowd's response to Jesus's ministry? Is something deeper being said here?
4. What images are used in 9:36-38 to describe Jesus's relationship with the people? What does this reveal to us about Jesus?
5. Why are these passages about Jesus good news for us today? How should they shape and inform how we live as Christ followers? (Focus particularly on Matt. 10:1.)

Chapter 2: If You Are Willing

1. Read Matthew 8:1-4 together. What leaps out at you? What questions do you have?

2. How would you describe the attitude of the man with leprosy toward Jesus? How might this shape the way we pray?

3. What is Jesus's attitude toward the man with leprosy?

4. In what ways does Jesus offer more than just physical healing in this encounter?

5. How may God's healing sometimes take a different form than what we are specifically asking for? Share times when you have experienced this in your own life.

6. Are there areas where you want to ask Jesus for healing? Do you believe He is willing? Are you open to receive the healing Jesus wants to give? Are you willing to receive life change beyond what you may be asking for? If appropriate, take time to pray for each other.

Chapter 3: Just Say the Word

1. Read Matthew 8:5-13. What leaps out at you? What questions do you have?

2. Darrell mentions that the centurion has faith in Jesus's compassion. What obstacles did he have to overcome to approach Jesus?

3. The centurion also had faith in Jesus's authority. How did he express this faith?

4. What does Darrell mean when he refers to "the

performative word"? Can you give examples of words that have made things happen in your life?

5. Where do you hear the word of God in your life? What rhythms could you build into your life to allow you to hear the word more frequently?

6. If you are comfortable in doing so, have a time of sharing your needs with one another. After a person has shared, allow a moment of silence, and then have the group pray together: "Just say the word, Lord, for if You do, something happens."

Chapter 4: He Takes and Carries

1. Read Matthew 8:14-17 together. What leaps out at you? What questions do you have?

2. How does Peter's mother-in-law respond to Jesus after He touches her? What is the significance of her response to Jesus?

3. What are the different types of healing that Jesus demonstrates in this passage?

4. Read Isaiah 53 together. As you reflect on Jesus's life, share the parts of this passage that stand out to you.

5. Why does Matthew mention Isaiah 53:4? What does this reveal to us about Jesus and His ministry?

6. "If you come to Jesus with your sickness, He will carry it. We can't be certain what He will do with it, but He'll carry our illnesses and diseases. You can come to Him with your filth, need, sickness—He takes it all." In light of this truth, take some time to pray for one another.

Chapter 5: Even the Wind and the Waves

1. Read Matthew 8:23-27. What leaps out at you? What questions do you have?

2. Describe a recent time when you felt like you were in over your head and about to go under. What did you do?

3. The disciples wake up Jesus with a cry. What do they say (see Mark 4:38)? What do they mean by this? Have you ever felt this way?

4. After Jesus calms the storm, the disciples ask in amazement, "Who is this?" How would you answer that question?

5. After Jesus calms the storm, He asks a question, "Where is your faith?" Think back over a recent crisis in your life (maybe to your answer to question #2). How would you answer Jesus's question?

Chapter 6: One Little Word Shall Fell Him

1. Read Matthew 8:28-34 together. What leaps out at you? What questions do you have?

2. What is the immediate response of the demons toward Jesus? What is surprising about how they address Jesus?

3. What does the demons' exchange with Jesus reveal about their attitude toward Him?

4. In Scripture, the word "behold" often signifies unexpected events or surprise. What surprises do the "beholds" reveal in these verses?

5. Discuss the town's response in verse 34. Why

may this be surprising?

6. How may this passage challenge our attitude toward the battle against the demonic? How is demonic illness a complicated or misunderstood issue in the church today?

7. Pray together as the Spirit leads.

Chapter 7: Authority to Forgive

1. Read Matthew 9:1-8 together. What leaps out at you? What questions do you have?

2. What does this passage have to teach us about the role of community in Jesus's healing ministry?

3. What is surprising about Jesus's immediate response to the paralyzed man? Why may this be different from what was expected?

4. Why was Jesus's response in verse 2 offensive to the Pharisees who were present?

5. Why is it easier to say, "Your sins are forgiven" than "Rise and walk?"

6. What is different about the healing that Jesus offers here compared to other passages we have looked at?

7. Take some time to pray together. Reflect on how God might be calling this community to partake in His healing ministry.

Chapter 8: Faith in the Valley of the Shadow of Death

1. Read Matthew 9:18-26 together. What leaps out at you? What questions do you have?

2. What are some of the parallels in this passage be-

tween the ruler and his daughter, and the bleeding woman? Why might these two accounts be
paired together?

3. What does the ruler's behavior in verse 18 reveal
about his attitude toward Jesus? What is Jesus's
response to the ruler?

4. What is the bleeding woman's attitude toward Jesus in verses 20-21? What is Jesus's response to the
woman?

5. What role does touch play in these two healings?

6. What can we learn from the account of the ruler
and the woman in this passage? How may we em-
ulate their faith in our own lives?

7. Together, pray for Jesus's healing touch on the
lives of those we know who are suffering.

Chapter 9: Just Keep Following Him Home

1. Read Matthew 9:27-34 together. What leaps out
at you? What questions do you have?

2. What different types of healing do we see in this
passage?

3. Why is the title by which the blind men address
Jesus significant (v. 27)?

4. Discuss Jesus's response in verse 29. What might
this imply about the relationship between faith
and healing?

5. Share areas of suffering/blindness in your own life
in which Jesus may be asking you, "Do you believe
that I am able to do this?"

QUESTIONS FOR SMALL GROUP STUDIES

6. Pray together that you would be given increased faith to answer, "Yes, Lord."

Chapter 10: Joining Jesus the Healer

1. Read Matthew 9:35-10:1 together. What leaps out at you? What questions do you have?

2. Review (from ch. 1) the images used in this passage that shed light on who Jesus is, and what He has come to do.

3. What are the needs that Jesus identifies in verses 35-38? How does Jesus meet these needs?

4. In what way does Jesus invite His followers to be an integral part of His healing ministry?

5. Matthew 10:1 states, "He gave them authority . . . " What does it look like to join Jesus the Healer? What does it mean to be a church with a healing ministry? Share personal experiences in this area.

6. Pray that God would empower and enable each individual, the group, and the church to live in the reality of this authority.

He Give Us a New Past!

1. Have five people read John 21:1-19 out loud for the group: the narrator; Peter; the other disciples (only in v. 3); the beloved disciple, John (only in v. 7); and Jesus. What was your reaction? What stood out to you this time?

2. Jesus shows up at the Sea of Galilee expressly to meet Peter. Why wait to meet him there? (Note

the similarities with Luke 5:1-11.)

3. Why is there a focus on the charcoal fire? What memory would it trigger for Peter? What does Jesus do around this fire?

4. What we see Jesus doing is what many call "the ministry of inner healing." Jesus meets us in the places of our past where we get stuck and heals that past in some way, freeing us from the "haunt" of it. Has He done this for you? And if so, could you briefly share the story with the group?

5. If you would like Him to do it for you, why not ask Him now? Name the place or event analogous to Peter's "charcoal fire." Then invite Jesus to meet you there, asking Him to heal the memory. Be still, and just listen and watch in your imagination. What do you sense Jesus saying or doing? This may take some time, so in the days to come, continue to invite Jesus to heal that stuck place. He will meet you there!

For Further Reading

Barclay, William. *The Gospel of Matthew: Volume 1 (Chapters 1-10)*, rev. ed. Philadelphia: Westminster, 1975.

Brown, Michael L. *Israel's Divine Healer*. Grand Rapids: Zondervan, 1995.

Bruner, F. Dale. *The Christbook: A Historical/Theological Commentary, Matthew 1-12*. Waco: Word Books, 1987.

MacNutt, Francis. *Healing*. Toronto: Bantam Books, 1974. (This is available in several editions. I prefer the 1974 edition.)

Norberg, Tilda and Robert D. Webber. *Stretch Out Your Hand: Exploring Healing Prayer*. Nashville: Upper Room, 1998.

Twelftree, Graham H. *Jesus the Miracle Worker: A Historical and Theological Study*. Downers Grove: IVP Academic, 1999.